BUILDING
YOUR HOME

BUILDING
YOUR HOME

a simple guide
to making
GOOD
DECISIONS

KRISTINA LEIGH WIGGINS

BROWN BOOKS
PUBLISHING GROUP

Building Your Home
A Simple Guide to Making Good Decisions

Brown Books Publishing Group
16250 Knoll Trail Drive, Suite 205
Dallas, Texas 75248
www.BrownBooks.com
(972) 381-0009

A New Era in Publishing®

ISBN 978-1-61254-940-8
LCCN 2016953172

Book design and initial editing by Larissa Wiese
www.KuramanCreative.com

Printed in the United States
10 9 8 7 6 5 4 3 2 1

Apple and the Apple logo are trademarks of Apple Inc., registered in the U.S. and other countries. App Store is a service mark of Apple Inc., registered in the U.S. and other countries.

App Store® is a trademark of Apple Inc., registered in the U.S. and other countries.

For more information or to contact the author, please go to www.SimplyKristinaLeigh.com

CONTENTS

Hello

In the many years I have been project managing homes, I have found that there is no good and simple guide to help people navigate the stressful waters of home building. There are tons of books and guides for other big life events such as weddings and having babies, but there are no helpful books to steer my clients through the pile of selections and decisions that they have to make when they are building their homes. As a result, I created a binder in triplicate that the client, the builder, and myself would each have to help keep everyone on the same page and the project moving. It also helped my clients to get a hold on the decisions and selections they need to make and to be prepared for the next step in a complex process. It stopped them from being overwhelmed by decisions. This book is the result of the many refinements to this incredible binder. So it is time to revamp this binder and bring it into the modern and digital world.

The goal of this guide is to simply and gently guide you on how to make good decisions when building a home. This book will help you break down the decisions you need to make into smaller parts so that you do not overwhelm yourself. Breaking things down into sections that are easy to tackle will help you to make good decisions by allowing you to focus on one thing at a time and not be consumed by what can seem like an insurmountable mountain of things that have to be determined during the process of home building. Staying clear and organized with the selections you have made is one of the hardest parts of building. The digital app that is a perfect complement to the book (called **Simpleigh Done** and available at the App Store®) is there to help you stay organized through this intense process they call building a home! We suggest you purchase this app early on in this process.

When you have made the giant decision to build a new home, the first thing you need to remember is that you are building a home for you and your family, not for your architect or your opinionated best friend. What *you* like is most important. It's not that "decision by committee" does not have its place (because it does and can often give great reassurance during the process), but you want to be careful to not muddy the waters by asking too many people what they think. It always helps to bounce ideas off someone if they are someone you really trust and know will have your best interest in mind. Try to identify who that person or persons are before you start the process so that you will have clarity of who to ask when you are having trouble landing on a decision.

Use the Simpleigh Done app to organize your decisions. ↗

ACKNOWLEDGMENTS

LARISSA WIESE OF KURAMAN CREATIVE

www.KuramanCreative.com

How can you ever adequately thank someone who helped take your dream and make it not only come to life but be more beautiful than you could have ever imagined! Thank you, Larissa, for capturing my vision by being an immensely talented person as well as a dear friend!

ROBERT AND MARY OF ROBERT RECK PHOTOGRAPHY AND JENNY WILDE OF SPRINKLE OF GRACE

www.RobertReck.com

SprinkleOfGrace.MyFotoJournal.com

I would like to thank Robert for his beautiful pictures of my designs and Jenny for her willingness to work with me on my pictures. The book would not be the same without your exquisite photos!

MARK AND LAURA OF MARK TODD ARCHITECTS AND KEVIN OF KEVIN SPEARMAN DESIGN GROUP

www.MWToddArch.com

www.KevinSpearman.com

I would like to thank Mark and Laura of Mark Todd Architects and Kevin of Kevin Spearman Design Group for taking a leap of faith by creating job positions for me—despite not having any openings—when I was fresh out of college and for teaching me the foundations of design.

MY EARLY CLIENTS

I would like to thank the early clients who put their trust in me—especially the Ainsworths, Luttrells, Culps, and McGraws—for not only allowing me to design their homes but also giving me the privilege of creating and managing every aspect of their homes during construction, resulting in lifelong friendships!

BROWN BOOKS PUBLISHING GROUP

Thank you to Brown Books for seeing the potential in my book and for guiding me through this crazy world they call publishing!

MY AMAZING FAMILY

Thank you to my family for their endless love and support. I am blessed beyond measure.

PROFESSIONALS

It takes countless skilled professionals to make a home come together. I would like to thank a few of the professionals who played key roles in some of the projects you see pictured in *Building Your Home*. Jamie of Ashingdon Homes; Chuck of Dawson Custom Homes; Milton of MR Lary Builder, Inc.; James and Julie of Van Stavern Interiors; Bree of Z Design at Home; Payam of Sarabi Studio; Jeremy and Jane of SGO Designer Glass; Amanda and Elliot of AG Lunson; Rock of Morrison's Supply; Ron and Gary of Bosworth; and Josh of Alldredge Gardens. Without the expertise and talent of these professionals, the homes featured would not be what they are, nor would the book.

1

SELECTING THE LOT

One of the most exciting steps in building a home is selecting your lot! This is when your dreams start to dance in your head. Until this moment you did not know that looking at a blank piece of property could be so darn exciting!

The best strategy is to have your lot selected before you start to design your home. A home design and lot layout should be in balanced harmony together, each a perfect complement for the other. One of the worst mistakes you can make is to force-fit a home design onto a lot.

Following are important exercises to do during the lot-finding process. It is a good idea to do this work whether you have eyed your treasured lot for years, or you are just starting the elusive search.

DRIVE, BABY, DRIVE

Traffic is an issue that can impact day-to-day life in a drastic way, so it is very important to have a firm grip and understanding of the traffic in that area. Several clients have known they were building spitting distance from a school or popular restaurant but assumed they were out of the path of congestion. This all comes to a head when they show up for a job-site meeting and realize that at certain times of the day or night their street becomes a parking lot. It is worth the time to do the reconnaissance!

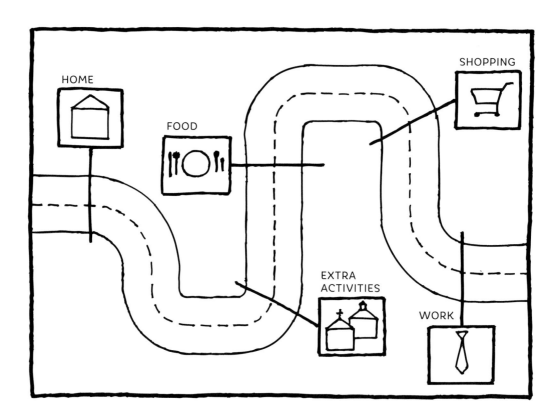

LOT SELECTION WORKSHEET

1 Drive to the lot in the morning **before** work, and start your commute to work from there.

Average morning commute

↓

TRIP ONE

minutes

TRIP TWO

minutes

TRIP THREE

minutes

_____ *minutes*

2 Drive to the lot **after** work during rush hour.

Average evening commute

↓

TRIP ONE

minutes

TRIP TWO

minutes

TRIP THREE

minutes

_____ *minutes*

IF YOU HAVE CHILDREN, CONTINUE ON TO STEP 3. OTHERWISE, SKIP TO STEP 6.

3

Drive to the lot in the early morning **before** school, and start your commute from there.

Average morning school commute

↓

TRIP ONE

minutes

TRIP TWO

minutes

TRIP THREE

minutes

_____ *minutes*

//////////////////////////////

Fair Warning:

This is a difficult task! To get the children to school on time without any extra diversions can require a great amount of kid wrangling. Add in an extra trip to the potential lot, and it can seem impossible. However, just push through the pain and do it! A few mornings of pain are far preferable to discovering major commute issues once you are married to it.

\\\\\\\\\\\\\\\\\\\\\\\\\\\\\\\

4

Drive to the lot **after** your children's school is out, and drive from school to there.

Average after school commute
↓

TRIP ONE
_____ minutes

TRIP TWO
_____ minutes

TRIP THREE
_____ minutes

---------------- *minutes*

5

Drive to the lot (if possible) **before** and **after** extracurricular activities.

Average other activities commute
↓

TRIP ONE
_____ minutes

TRIP TWO
_____ minutes

TRIP THREE
_____ minutes

---------------- *minutes*

6

Drive to the lot after a heavy rain. Describe the conditions below.

TRIP ONE

TRIP TWO

TRIP THREE

What is the general state of the streets around your lot after a rain, and how is your lot with regards to flooding?

STATE OF STREETS (Circle one).

OVERALL STATE IN POOR WEATHER

....

....

....

....

....

....

....

....

Are there any other places you regularly visit? Perhaps the grocery store, dry cleaner, bank, friends' and families' houses, babysitter, church, and doctors' offices. Repeat the exercise at an appropriate time of day for each location. Note your findings on the next the page.

ACTIVITY 1

TRIP ONE

minutes

TRIP TWO

minutes

TRIP THREE

minutes

Activity 1 commute

↓

ACTIVITY 2

TRIP ONE

minutes

TRIP TWO

minutes

TRIP THREE

minutes

Activity 2 commute

↓

RESEARCH

Put on your lab coat, and get into research mode! You will want to investigate the following potential location issues. They can have a significant effect on your property value, regardless of whether they affect your everyday life.

FUTURE DEVELOPMENT

If at all possible, do not be the first to build in a new area. If it really is your best option to buy a lot in an undeveloped neighborhood, go to the city, and find out if there is a master plan for the area. This will help you to know if a future main road or highway, stadium, apartments, or other structures will ever be built right behind you.

What did you find on future development?

CRIME

Determine the amount of crime that takes place in and around that area. CrimeMapping.com is a good website to visit to locate this information.

What did you find on crime?

SCHOOL

Determine the school district ratings. Do this exercise whether you have children or not, as it will play a role in your resale value. A good website to visit is GreatSchools.org.

What did you find on school ratings?

DEEDS

Determine what type of deeds are in place for that lot and who enforces them.

Deeds are always specific to neighborhoods and can tell you things such as the size of home allowed, what materials can be used, paint colors allowed, whether pets are allowed, and the like.

To get a copy of the deeds you will need to contact the Homeowners' Association or request a copy from the seller of the lot.

What did you find on the deeds?

///////////////////////////

Quick Note:

Deeds are generally available from the Homeowners' Association. They are rules and regulations with regard to use of land, the look of the lot and neighborhood, and the maintenance of the homes.

\\\\\\\\\\\\\\\\\\\\\\\\\\\\

HOMEOWNERS' ASSOCIATION

Determine what type of homeowners' association is in place and what fees are charged annually.

What did you find on homeowners' fees?

NEIGHBORS

If the area you are looking in is an area that is already developed, find people who live there, and do not be afraid to ask questions like:

"How do you like living here?"

"Have you been surprised by anything?"

"How is the traffic?"

"Are there any block parties?"

What did you find out from existing neighbors?

PROPERTY VALUES

Determine the property values of the homes around your potential lot, and make sure that you are within the same range. One of the easiest ways to give you a quick idea of the property values it to look at a real estate website and see the value of the homes that are for sale or have just recently sold. You do not want to be the most expensive house in the neighborhood.

What did you find out about property values?

 SPEND TIME ON THE LOT

Stand on the lot and ask yourself these questions:

1

What is the best view from the lot?

....

....

....

....

....

2

How is the view from the front of the lot looking toward the rear?

Are there any views you want to maximize or hide?

....

....

....

....

....

3

How is the view from the back of the lot looking toward the front?
Are there any views you want to maximize or hide?

....

....

....

....

4

How does the sun affect the lot in the morning?

....

....

....

....

5

How does the sun affect the lot in the afternoon?

....

....

....

....

6   *How does the sun affect the lot in the evening?*

There are a number of programs and apps you can use to determine sun direction and shadow length across your lot without having to stand there twenty-four hours a day. The most economical is the free **SunCalc** website at SunCalc.net. A pricier but more user-friendly option is the **Helios Sun and Moon Position Calculator**, which you can find at the App Store.

Use the space below to draw the sun direction on your lot in the morning, afternoon, and evening.

7 *Are there any two-storey homes looking directly into your lot?*

_____

_____

_____

8 *Is there any established landscape?*

_____

_____

_____

_____

Draw any important landscape features below.

9   *Is your lot big enough—does it have the proper amount of space to grow on and satisfy all of your master plan dreams? Master planning will be described in more detail on page 119.*

....

....

....

....

....

10   *What is your favorite attribute of this lot? (Examples include cost, location, neighborhood, style of neighborhood, or view.)*

....

....

....

....

If you are looking at a few options and are having a problem deciding on a lot, use the following form to help you do direct comparisons between your options.

LOT COMPARISON WORKSHEET

	LOT 1	LOT 2	LOT 3
MORNING COMMUTE	minutes	minutes	minutes
EVENING COMMUTE	minutes	minutes	minutes
MORNING SCHOOL COMMUTE	minutes	minutes	minutes
AFTERNOON COMMUTE	minutes	minutes	minutes
EXTRACURRICULAR COMMUTE	minutes	minutes	minutes
STATE OF LOT AFTER HEAVY RAIN	☺ ☺ ☹	☺ ☺ ☹	☺ ☺ ☹
FUTURE DEVELOPMENT			
CRIME STATISTICS			
SCHOOL DISTRICT RATINGS			

	LOT 1	LOT 2	LOT 3
DEEDS			
HOA			
FUTURE NEIGHBOR FEEDBACK			
PROPERTY VALUES			
VIEWS FROM LOT			
SUN ON LOT			
LANDSCAPE			
FAVORITE ATTRIBUTE			
COST			
PREFERRED LOT			

CONGRATULATIONS ON FINDING YOUR PERFECT LOT!

Fill out the information about the lot you landed on.

The legal description of the lot (make sure you have a drawing of the site plan).

PREPARE YOUR RELATIONSHIP FOR BUILDING

So you have found your lot and decided, "Yes—we are going for it!" This is not only a very exciting time in the process but also a perfect time to start preparing your relationship for the oh-so-stressful craziness we call building a new home. Now, I do not want to seem like a "Debbie Downer," but building a house can really put a strain on a couple's relationship and even strain other relationships close to you.

One of the biggest ways to create a successful project is to always be prepared ahead of time with your decisions and selections. The same rule applies to your relationship: be prepared! I want to help you prepare by putting in perspective the different phases of home building in terms of the process that we are all pretty familiar with—getting married. The phases of building are very much like a wedding.

The Engagement

You decide that you are going to build a house and start looking for the lot!

The Wedding

You close on the lot, you seal the deal.

The Honeymoon

The early stages of design and day dreaming together about your lot and all of its wonderful possibilities.

The honeymoon ends and reality sets in

Construction begins.

You start to learn the highs and lows of living together

The whole construction process.

You live happily ever after

The construction of your new home ends, and you move in.

Just like in life, I am sorry to say that the honeymoon does not last long. When I was a project manager I would say one of my biggest roles (aside from being the middle man between the client and builder) was being the middle man between a husband and a wife. I was constantly striving to make a very stressful situation less stressful on a marriage. I remember being fresh out of college and sitting down to review some floor plan decisions with my clients and—wham! An argument ensues right before my eyes. My first thoughts were, "Oh gosh, they did not teach you this in college. Marriage Counseling 101, where were you when I needed you?!"

So, over the next several years it became clearer and clearer (after the umpteenth fight I quietly sat through until it reached a good stopping point) that, sure, building may be stressful on your bank account and be a vacuum on your time, but the stress on your marriage and family or relationships is the silent predator you do not see coming! So, time to prepare for taking steps to ready your marriage and relationships for building!

Here are a few tips for getting prepared:

1. HAVE YOUR LOVE TANKS FULL BEFORE YOU BEGIN CONSTRUCTION

Seriously, gas that puppy up!

2. BUILDING HAS THREE MAIN COMPONENTS

1 How much is it going to cost?

2 How long will it take?

3 What will it look like?

Determine what component is most important to each of you. Are you:

COST FOCUSED
"Budget Betty" or *"Finance Frank"*

TIMELINE FOCUSED
"Punctual Patty" or *"Prompt Pedro"*

STYLE FOCUSED
"Appearance Ava" or *"Design Dan"*

Looking at these funny names might seem like a silly exercise, but they will really help to start opening up the dialog about what is most important to you and how to respect what is most important to the other person. If you are an "Appearance Ava" who cares most about design but are married to a "Finance Frank" who care little about the design and a lot about how much it cost, this will help you to communicate better. When "Appearance Ava" is making a tile selection and found a tile in budget that she really likes but a tile she really loves that is out of budget, she should think about her "Finance Frank" and if it is worth the stress and conflict that might arise over spending a lot more money on something that is only a little bit better. And vice versa. If you are a "Finance Frank," do not draw a hard line and refuse to give a little if "Appearance Ava" found a carpet she loves that is just a touch more costly and is important to her. Identifying what is most important to you will help you to respect each other's wants and land on successful compromises.

3. DETERMINE YOUR PERSONALITY TYPES

At this point, just take your best guess, but be prepared that you may evolve when the process actually gets underway, and you can always reassess. I have seen with my own eyes a "Bold Becky" become a "Cannot Decide Connie." Are you . . .

↘ **EAGER**
"Excited Ella" or *"Energized Eric"*

↘ **INDECISIVE**
"Cannot Decide Connie" or *"Not Sure Nick"*

↘ **AGGRESSIVE**
"Bold Becky" or *"Pushy Pete"*

↘ **PASSIVE**
"Accommodating Amy" or *"Compliant Carl"*

↘ **RELAXED**
"Nonchalant Nikki" or *"Laid-Back Larry"*

↘ **NERVOUS**
"Tense Tina" or *"Jumpy Jack"*

↘ **RELUCTANT**
"Don't Want To Do It Danielle" or *"Not A Fan Nathan"*

↘ **INDIFFERENT**
"Whatever Whitney" or *"I Don't Care Ivan"*

The way different personalities work on a job site is always very interesting. I have seen it where there is a whole lot of "Accommodating Amys" and "Laid-Back Larrys" and decisions are hard to come by. If you are two eager beavers who want to build, there will be far more extreme highs and lows because of your passion, but the excitement for you both when you cross the finish line and move into your new home will be blissful.

4. DETERMINE YOUR ROLES

One of the keys to avoiding stress is to determine what items are most important to you, what role you will play in the process, and the same for anyone else involved. By having these discussions before decisions have to be made and when you are not under pressure, you can hopefully talk about it without launching verbal grenades at each other. If you have not clearly defined your roles this can lead to major conflict down the road. Waiting until you are in the middle of building to discuss them will cause the stress level to get high, and the verbal grenades will start to explode. Building requires a lot of time and energy, and having a clear plan in place will ease the tensions. Here is a recent true story of two of my clients.

Her: We need a plan. You have a huge project at work and I'm managing a huge project in this new house. How are we going to survive this?!

Him: We aren't. I'm just going to jump off the new dormer.

Her: Well, that's a problem, because it won't kill you. It will only disable you, making you more dependent on me. And I don't have time for that.

Then they started laughing so hard the argument ended.

It would sure be blissful if you really could just split the roles down the middle, but the truth of the matter is that you both will play some part in every role—even if you are not the lead role. Be sure when you are determining your roles that you keep in mind what causes you the most stress. If you are an "Accommodating Amy" and the idea of having to let your builder know you are unhappy with something sends you in a panic, then you are probably best off just being the understudy in that role. If you are a "Finance Frank" and the idea of not knowing exactly where things stand on costs makes you start sweating, then you better take the lead role on finances. By sitting down and discussing what stresses you out most, it will allow you to come up with a plan that best fits your unique situation.

CHOOSE YOUR ROLES

Lead role for communicating with builder ....

Understudy for communicating with builder ....

Lead role for communicating with architect ....

Understudy for communicating with architect ....

Lead role for communicating with designer ....

Understudy for communicating with designer ....

Lead role for finances ....

Understudy for finances ....

Lead role for selections ....

Understudy for selections ....

Lead role for on-site meetings ....

Understudy for on-site meetings ....

Again, by determining ahead of time what lead role you will each take, it will make the waters ahead much less murky.

5. ATTEND ALL INITIAL MEETINGS TOGETHER

Here is a classic story: only one spouse attends the meeting. They go home to translate the meeting, but the translation does not go well. The nonattender thinks they did not land on the best option, but the attender knows they did because they attended and heard directly from the designer's mouth the "whys" behind the options.

Save yourself lots of headache, and attend all initial meetings together. I have run into it over and over again: one person says, "You know, this is not as big a deal to me. I just want to live in it!" They may genuinely feel that way, but they are telling tall tales without realizing it. When it boils down to it, *everyone* has an opinion about what they live in. You may have a stronger opinion on the cost of the item versus the aesthetics, but you have it. In my many years of doing this I have only ever encountered one person who had a spouse that literally did not care. If she arrived to a job-site meeting, it was only because she had a question for her husband about something totally not related. It was hysterical. If this is you, go out for ice cream. If you do not have this kind of one-in-a-million relationship, attending all initial meetings together will make the process a much smoother one. Once you get into a rhythm as the project goes (like when you get to the Big Details), it is less vital to both attend, and your lead roles and understudy roles will start to take hold. If you find you are running into a lot of resistance from your counterpart on attending the first handful of meetings, I would sign two simple contracts that state:

If you do not attend the initial meetings, you forfeit your vote!

(sign here)

If I do not see the need to attend the meeting, I forfeit my vote!

.... *(sign here)*

It may seem like an extreme suggestion, but by the third meeting you attend as the process starts that your other half does not which leads to frustration, confusion, and blow-ups, you will probably revisit this simple contract and ask for signatures. You may even want to get the signature notarized at that point!

CONCLUSION

I cannot emphasize enough: the best way to avoid the most tension in a highly stressful situation is to give yourself plenty of time to work through your decisions and have open discussions about what it most important to you in this process and what causes you the most anxiety. I know this is easier said than done, and inevitably you will find yourself in a stressful situation, but use your app, stay organized, and stay ahead of the game! This will preserve your sanity and your relationships. And even when the situation might get tense between the two of you, ask yourself if the situation at hand is a tragedy. If it is a tragedy, which would be a rarity, then it is understandable if you totally break down. But if it is not a tragedy, then it is just irritation or inconvenience, so calm down, and remember that you love each other enough to want to be under the same roof of a new house together, day in and day out, from this point forward . . . So this too shall pass!

2

DETERMINE YOUR STYLE

Before you jump into starting plans (plans are addressed more specifically in chapter 5), I think it is important to make choices regarding some important features of the home.

Determine your style. It doesn't have to be a strict description, and it may evolve as your plans evolve, but it is important to at least make a first run at it.

The best way to narrow in on your style is to find inspirational images of pictures of homes you just love and could move right into. You can find these images by searching the amazing website Houzz.com—it has endless amounts of inspirational images for you to search. Be sure to not only store your images on the Houzz.com website, but also store them in your app. For some of you a picture is just not as good as seeing a home in person. If this is the case, you need to drive around your own town (or on every one of your out-of-town trips) and snap pictures of homes you see that you love.

You will want to locate two or three inspirational images for all parts of your home inside and out. One thing you will want to be careful of is not to overwhelm yourself with too much inspiration. It is fine initially to collect ten or more pictures of kitchens or bathrooms that you love, but when it is time to really start narrowing in on your final decisions you will want to only have a top two or three images that you will refer back to often. You can store these photos in the sister app for your book. As you are making design decisions you will want to consult back to these images to make sure you are staying in line with your sweet spots. Sometimes what may also happen over the process of making your selections and building your home is that your taste may evolve. As your style evolves be sure and let the old inspirations and directions go (delete them) so that you do not find yourself pulled in too many directions. It will be hard—but narrow down, narrow down, narrow down, so that the inspiration images you are using as reference are really the top, most-prized ones.

EXTERIOR

Determining the style of your exterior (or outside) of your house will usually set the stage for all other elements of the house. For example, a description of one of my projects was a modern farmhouse with stone (shown above).

There are many types of exterior styles, and you will need to do your research to find the style that suits you and your family. As mentioned previously, a great resource for learning about house style is Houzz.com. Some of the following house styles are used on Houzz.com. Take the time to visit the website to study the styles and then circle the styles from the list below that appeal to you.

EXTERIOR STYLE WORKSHEET

Circle any exterior house styles below that appeal to you.

CONTEMPORARY   ECLECTIC   MODERN   TRADITIONAL   ASIAN

BEACH STYLE   CRAFTSMAN   FARMHOUSE   INDUSTRIAL   MEDITERRANEAN

MIDCENTURY   RUSTIC   SOUTHWESTERN   TRANSITIONAL   TROPICAL

TEXAS HILL COUNTRY   FRENCH COUNTRY   VICTORIAN   PLANTATION   ITALIANTE

COTTAGE   LOG CABIN   QUEENSLANDER   BIG CITY FLAT   SCANDINAVIAN

INTERIOR

Determining your interior style is so important because you spend most of your time interacting with the house on the inside. The interior is the heartbeat of the house. It is what gives you that sense of home—and the comfort being home.

INTERIOR STYLE WORKSHEET

Here is a list of words to help you determine your interior style. Tick all that apply.

INTERIOR STYLES		
	☐ PRIVATE	☐ OPEN
	☐ FORMAL	☐ CASUAL
	☐ MODERN	☐ CLASSIC
	☐ WARM/INVITING	☐ VINTAGE
	☐ CLEAN LINES	☐ MINIMALIST
	☐ COLLECTOR	☐ FUN
	☐ SERIOUS	☐ RUSTIC
	☐ BRIGHT	☐ DARK
	☐ CONTEMPORARY	

Now, take all of the words you circled and fill in the sentence below. For example, "My house will be a midcentury modern exterior with a classic interior that has open spaces," or "My house will be a rustic farmhouse exterior with a classic and bright contemporary interior."

My house is a:

\---

\---

\---

\---

\---

3
DETERMINE THE BIGGIES

Once you have determined your style it is time to tackle what I call "the biggies." These are not only big-ticket items with regard to cost, but very important things to know before you start your plans. In particular, they are essential to have a handle on before you meet with your builder. All of the "biggies" are listed below and are broken down into individual topics over the next several pages.

Remember that the goal right now is to start narrowing in on the things you like. You may have two or three things listed for each "biggie item." Once you start to work on plans and get firm numbers back on the budget, these decisions will start to come a little easier.

If you are going to enlist the help of a professional designer, get a subscription to the LUXE magazine for your region and join Houzz.com. Visit their websites to get information on great designers in your area. A professional designer can help you to determine this list, but do not fear if a professional designer is out of budget. By breaking it down into smaller components you can tackle this list yourself.

THE BIGGIES ARE . . .

→ *Exterior vertical materials*
....

→ *Roof*
....

→ *Front door*
....

→ *Windows*
....

→ *Garage doors*
....

→ *Exterior jewelry*
....

→ *Landscape*
....

→ *Driveway*
....

Fill in your own biggies list on page 72. Here is what your biggies list might look like:

Exterior vertical materials

Leaning toward stone but open to brick if stone cost is too high

Roof

Metal roof

Front door

Thinking wood but open to iron

Windows

Dark windows that have a bungalow feel

Garage doors

Solid color, painted

Exterior jewelry

Planter baskets and a flag pole

Landscape

Lots of flowering trees and bushes

Driveway

Pavers but open to plain concrete if too expensive

EXTERIOR MATERIALS

There are lots of factors to consider when picking exterior materials. From style to climate conditions, to cost to deed restrictions—you name it. The style you determine for your home will most likely dictate what type of exterior material you will choose. If you desire a Mediterranean feel, you may lean toward stucco or plaster, whereas a rustic home may lend itself toward natural stone and reclaimed wood siding. Either way, keep in mind that this material will become the backdrop for all the other elements you use on the exterior. Do not be afraid to mix materials. For example, mixing dry stack stone with large boulders of the same stone or stone with stucco can create a unique look.

Some parts of a house are easy to upgrade or change further down the road, but exterior materials are not. Budget enough money to make a good selection on the exterior materials so you have a good solid base to work from.

A word of caution: mixing fake materials such as cultured stone and vinyl with real materials such as real stone and wood siding can be difficult. Often the real material will steal the show and make your fake material look cheap. Keep this in mind if you are building in a neighborhood that has lots of homes with authentic stone or brick as it can make your replica stone or brick look cheesy in comparison. If you are using cultured stone for anything more substantial than the base of a column, I urge you to go with the real thing. There are a handful of well-done cultured stones out there that can fool almost anybody—but they are few and far between. The same goes with stucco foam molds that are made to look like cast stone surrounds. There are some who can make stucco foam molds look amazing—but the vast majority cannot. I would encourage you to use no foam surrounds or trim out fewer windows (perhaps use cast or carved stone on just a few key windows). As with any material, you have to consider both aesthetics and maintenance. Let's take wood, for example. There is great character that comes with real wood siding that you just cannot achieve with vinyl siding; but there is also an issue of maintenance that (depending on what climate you are building in) may require annual work. Sometimes function will rightfully trump aesthetics, but in those cases, the details you put on the exterior will become even more crucial.

It is also important that, as you start narrowing down your exterior material options, you go and visit homes with the same type of material. You should see it en masse before you make your final selection. A stone, brick, or stucco color may look very different in a photograph or on a 12-inch-square sample board so ask the distributor you end up working with to guide you to homes that have used it. If no homes in your area have that material that is okay. Still keep it as an option on the table, and put it up on your sample wall to determine if it is a good option for your home. A sample wall is a wall generally as small as 2 feet wide and 4 feet tall with a small framed roof on it (if you are pretty sure you know what material you want). However, it may be as big as 10 feet wide and 4 feet tall with a small framed roof on it (if you are trying to choose between several materials). Samples of this nature are always a small added expense but are imperative to a successful process. This sample wall allows you to see your exterior materials and trim as well as roofing material all together. They arm you with the visual you need to make a good decision.

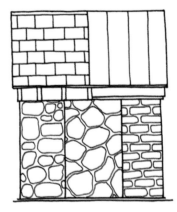

SAMPLE WALL

EXTERIOR MATERIAL WORKSHEET

Remember that you are not trying to pick just one. Tick all that apply.

EXTERIOR MATERIAL EXAMPLES		
	☐ STONE	☐ CULTURED STONE
	☐ BRICK	☐ CULTURED BRICK
	☐ STUCCO	☐ PLASTER
	☐ VINYL SIDING	☐ CEMENT BOARD SIDING
	☐ WOOD SIDING	☐ WOOD SHAKE
	☐ RECLAIMED WOOD SIDING	☐ METAL SIDING
	☐ TILE	☐ CAST STONE
	☐ CONCRETE	☐ OTHER

ROOF

The roof material is very important to the character of a home. A clay tile roof will immediately set the stage for something Mediterranean, whereas a metal roof might be just the thing to give a home a modern edge. Roof materials vary largely depending on location due to environmental needs, so be sure when you are researching your roof options that you do not fall in love with a material that is not available for your region. Once you have picked a few options you like, talk to the distributor and ask them for addresses of homes in the area you can go visit for reconnaissance. It is imperative that you see the roof en masse before you jump in the deep end. It is also very important that you know what roof material you are leaning toward, because it will affect the structural drawings of your home plans. Also, keep in mind that the roof is often one place worth the splurge because the cost of a very energy-efficient roof can be returned quickly via savings on your utility bills. For example, the first home I lived in in West Texas was a 2,700-square-foot thirty-year-old home with a composition roof and standard insulation. It had one AC unit and our electricity bills were often over $400 per month. Compare that to our new home. It is almost 8,000 square feet with spray-in foam insulation and a corrugated metal roof. The roof has an insulated air gap and five air conditioning units. Our electricity bills now generally fall between $250 and $300. The upgrades can pay out quickly and save money in the long run. Also keep in mind that a roof can always be changed if the proper structurals on the house are in place. The structurals on a house are the framing members that support the weight and structure of the house. These are generally determined by an engineer for both the foundation and framing of the house. For example, the size and type and spacing of framing is very different for a slate roof than it is for a composition roof. If you plan to one day upgrade from a composition roof to a slate roof make sure that this is noted on the construction documents so that the foundation and framing are properly engineered to carry the weight of the slate. If you really want a slate roof, but can only afford composition in the near term—think big! Plan to live with composition until you can afford slate and upgrade. Remember, master planning is always a wise thing to do. See page 119 for more on master planning.

ROOF MATERIAL WORKSHEET

Below are some examples of exterior material choices available. Tick the roof material(s) you are leaning toward:

ROOF MATERIAL EXAMPLES				
	☐	COMPOSITION: ROLL	☐	COMPOSITION: 3-TAB
	☐	COMPOSITION: HIGH DEFINITION	☐	METAL: CORRUGATED
	☐	METAL: STANDING SEAM	☐	SLATE
	☐	CONCRETE TILE	☐	CLAY TILE
	☐	SYNTHETIC CLAY TILE	☐	METAL SHINGLE
	☐	WOOD SHAKE	☐	OTHER

Quick Tip:

If you are unsure of what roof you like, visit Houzz.com and search for pictures of these roofs.

FRONT DOOR

You have probably heard the saying "the eyes are a window into the soul." The front door to a house is quite similar—it is the gateway to the soul of the house. The front door is a great place to set the stage for your home. If you want your house to have a quirky edge, then add a little funk to your front door. If you want to have a tone of sophistication to your home, then a highly formalized door might be your best bet. There is now also a great market for using reclaimed doors. This can add a sense of depth to a home that is hard to match.

Regardless of what type of style you are leaning toward, there are important factors to consider when making this selection. The questions below will help guide you to determine if you want a grand glass door or a charming solid wood door.

Is privacy important to you? If so, a solid or mostly solid door would be a good choice.

Is natural light or visibility out the front door important to you? If so, a mostly glass door would be a good choice.

Does your environment make it possible that your door may be exposed to extreme sun or rain? If so, an all-weather door may be a good choice.

DOOR MATERIAL WORKSHEET

Tick the front door material(s) you are leaning toward:

FRONT DOOR MATERIALS		
	☐ SOLID	☐ WOOD
	☐ IRON	☐ COLORED GLASS
	☐ PARTIAL-GLASS	☐ CLEAR GLASS
	☐ TREATED GLASS (e.g. WATER GLASS, SEATED GLASS)	☐ PAINTED
	☐ STAINED	☐ CHARMING
	☐ GRAND	☐ SINGLE
	☐ DOUBLE	☐ OTHER

Think about those first few steps after you walk inside your new front door. What do you want to see? Is there a specific view of the lot? Would you like people to enter a private foyer? Do you want people to enter an open living space? Take the time to ponder this scenario, and determine what you want to see on the other side of your front door.

I want to see (fill in the blank):

- -

- -

when both myself and my guests walk through the front door.

Often people never use their front door. Their real "front door" is the door between the garage and the house, or the carport and the house. If this is the case, be sure to think about this "front door"—as well as your main one, and what you want to see upon entry. It may be a mud room, a junk drop, or a capturing view as well.

I want to see (fill in the blank):

- -

- -

when myself and my guests walk through my personal front door.

FRONT DOOR WORKSHEET

Circle any front door styles below that appeal to you. As there are so many styles to choose from, these sketches are here to kick-start your imagination.

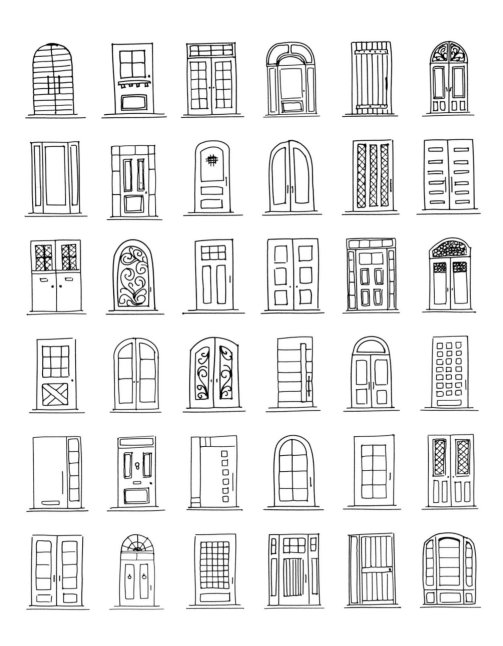

WINDOWS

Windows can really have an impact on both the aesthetics of a house and your building budget! Some things are easy to change (such as your roof material or exterior fixtures), but some things are not. Windows are extremely costly, and it is difficult to alter their shape and size once they are installed.

In my opinion, very few things can compare to the design impact windows have on a house. They allow natural light to fill dark spaces and give character to a room that cannot be described. There are also endless forms, shapes, and styles with windows. The sky is the limit!

Do not be afraid to mix different types of windows. One of my favorite combinations is a mix of vibrant leaded glass with other windows to give added excitement to a space. I also very often mix a few key all-wood windows that are paintable a fun color. They pop against the landscape of other windows on both the interior and exterior of the home.

If the thought of determining what type of window is overwhelming, do not fret. Just wait until you have selected a builder and they can give you guidance on what types of windows are good for your area, and the costs associated with the windows. If not, I would visit several window dealers in your area and quiz them on the pros and cons of each type of window.

The following page shows a number of different window options, categorized into divided light windows, picture windows, and mixed windows.

DIVIDED LIGHT
WINDOWS

PICTURE
WINDOWS

MIXED
WINDOWS

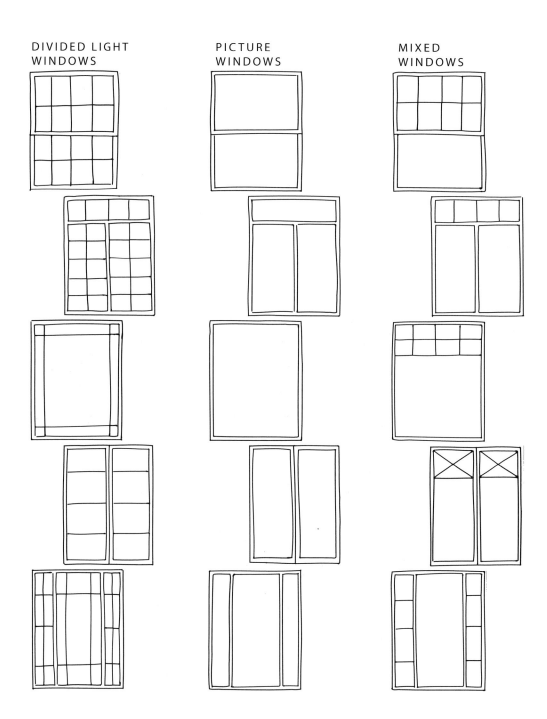

WINDOW MATERIAL WORKSHEET

Here are the most common window types. What material of window do you want to pursue?

WINDOW				
	☐	VINYL	☐	COMPOSITE
	☐	ALUMINUM-CLAD OUTSIDE & WOOD INSIDE	☐	ALL-WOOD WINDOW
	☐	IRON WINDOW	☐	LEADED GLASS
	☐	TEXTURED GLASS	☐	STAINED

On a side note, I did not mention glass block—and there is a reason why. For the love of Pete, please do not use it! True, it is functional by both letting natural light in and creating privacy, but its time in the spotlight is gone. Please don't date your house by putting in glass block!

SCREENS

What type of screens do you want?

SCREEN				
	☐	FIXED	☐	RETRACTABLE

GARAGE DOORS

Garage doors are an interesting feature in a home because the effort you put into them is generally directly tied to their location in the home. If the garage doors are positioned front and center, then their aesthetic importance is paramount. If the doors are tucked in on the side of the house (or around the back) then they become a place to really save money. The restrictions on your lot may dictate your choice here. Some deeds will state that no garage doors can face the street, while others will speak against any rear entries. Be sure and determine what your deeds say on this matter before you make a decision on the garage doors.

My deeds state that the garage doors:

Garage doors choices generally fall into two categories—you can choose a basic door or a decorative door.

Basic garage doors

Decorative garage doors

GARAGE DOORS

Determine which style of garage door you want to explore:

GARAGE DOOR	☐ BASIC	☐ DECORATIVE

EXTERIOR FIXTURES

Curb Appeal:

How attractive your house is from the street. If you were driving down the street, does a house catch your eye because it is appealing to you, or does it grab your attention because it is awful? It is a helpful practice to drive through neighborhoods and take notes on houses that catch your eye for both good and bad reasons.

The curb appeal of a house is often determined by the exterior fixtures you put on it. A house may have a good base structure but will not come to life until you add just the perfect gas lights and planter baskets. Each fixture has its own special style that can reinforce your exterior choices, but regardless of which style you are constructing, determine what the details are in advance so that they can be incorporated into the front elevation drawings.

EXTERIOR FIXTURES

Use the sketches below to get thinking about the type of exterior fixtures that you will use. Once you have decided, tick off the relevant fixtures on the next page.

LIGHTING FIXTURES SHUTTERS AWNINGS PLANTER BASKET GATES

PLANTERS CORBELS COLUMNS DECORATIVE IRON FOUNTAINS

CHIMNEY TOPPERS DORMERS CAST STONE SURROUNDS CAST STONE HEADERS MAILBOXES

TIMBER HEADERS WEATHER VANE PLANTER POTS FLAGPOLES CUPOLAS

HOUSE NUMBERS GUTTERS DORMER VENTS BALCONIES GABLED VENTS

EXTERIOR FIXTURES WORKSHEET

**EXTERIOR
DETAILS**

☐ LIGHT FIXTURES   ☐ SHUTTERS

☐ AWNINGS   ☐ PLANTER BASKETS

☐ GATES   ☐ PLANTERS

☐ CORBELS   ☐ COLUMNS

☐ DECORATIVE IRON   ☐ FOUNTAINS

☐ CHIMNEY TOPPERS   ☐ DORMERS

☐ CAST STONE   ☐ MAILBOXES
  SURROUNDS
  AND HEADERS

☐ TIMBER HEADERS   ☐ WEATHER VANES

☐ PLANTER POTS   ☐ FLAG STANDS OR
                            POLE

☐ CUPOLAS   ☐ HOUSE NUMBERS

☐ GUTTERS   ☐ DORMER VENTS

☐ BALCONIES   ☐ GABLED VENTS

LANDSCAPE

If you are one of the lucky ones that has a lot with big beautiful trees and established greenery—embrace it! Keep in mind that at every turn you are designing your floor plan. Those giant established trees are a gift that should be considered an immovable piece of art. However, if you are in the majority and have a pretty blank slate with regard to landscape, don't be disheartened. The only thing holding you back is your imagination (and the climate and budget too!). Often the landscape doesn't come into play until the end of the construction process—which is when you have generally broken the budget, so it gets drastically cut and cut until you end up with a front yard of just grass and one small planted tree. If landscape is important to you, you must be very disciplined to stay within budget during the construction. Then, when you are at the finish line, you do not have to forgo an important biggie to you and be greatly disappointed. If landscape is not that important to you, then this is a great place to master plan and use your budget to tackle your hot buttons first and landscape later. Ultimately though, landscape is key to great design (and great landscape can go a long way for covering up bad design). There is just something about nature that cannot be replicated. It creates a beauty that just moves something within you. It just moves you when you see it. Nature was created with immense variety. She can be spectacular and her spectrum is infinite—from lush forests to colorful cactus gardens. Regardless of what type landscape you choose, one of the most important considerations is the type of climate you are building in. Landscape is expensive to put in and costly to maintain—especially if you are fighting against nature. If you try to plant a forest in the desert, you are going to be in for a long and hard fight that you could lose. Visit local nurseries and ask lots of questions to learn about which plants and trees do well in your area (and which ones do not). This will help you to make an educated decision in the long run versus choosing foliage that looks pretty or interesting.

LANDSCAPING WORKSHEET

Is the maintenance level high or low?

Does it have established trees?

Does it need any new trees?

What types of grass does it currently contain?

Does it have any of the following?

☐ Turf

☐ Rock

☐ Crushed granite

☐ Hard surfaces such as driveways and sidewalks

☐ Planters

☐ Raised planters

☒

☐ Garden space

☐ Playgrounds

☐ Swimming pools

☐ Sport court

☐ Outdoor fireplace

Write a summary of what your landscape needs are:

BIGGIES LIST PRIORITISED

Now that you have given thought to all of the biggies it is time to get your priorities in line! Take time to fill in the list with your list of biggies in monetary priority with #1 being most important and #7 being least important.

Choose from:

→ *Exterior vertical materials*

→ *Roof*

→ *Front door*

→ *Windows*

→ *Garage doors*

→ *Exterior jewelry*

→ *Landscape*

Although the dollar signs may not really be an exact indication of how much you will spend on each item, it is a visual to help you figure out in your head the items you are willing to splurge on and get the best and the items you are not so willing to bust open the bank for.

THE BIGGIES PRIORITIZED BY BUDGET

1 $ _____

2 $ _____

3 $ _____

4 $ _____

5 $ _____

6 $ _____

7 $ _____

4

PAINT, OH, PAINT!?!

Time to pick paint? At this point you are busy making selections on your biggies (and nailing it I am sure!), and you are peeking ahead to see all of the decisions that you have to make down the road, like cabinets, texture, and trim . . . and it hits you. All of a sudden you realize that among all of these hard decisions you are getting ready to make on cabinet design, trim, walls, and ceiling is another decision: PAINT. What the heck, right? Paint always seems to be that unexpected piñata ball of stress that is just waiting to explode during the project. You know when you see the disclaimer on TV, "Do not try this at home"? That same disclaimer should come with picking paint . . . even experts have a hard time! But here is the good news: it is not time for the piñata to bust on your head and pelt you in the noggin. It is not time to pick paint! Far from it—phew! I just added this section to make sure that you do not worry yourself about paint right now. The paint decisions are coming, but no need to add stress to your life pondering them now! Over the next few weeks you will be making all of your decisions on tile, trim, plumbing, appliances, and so forth, but do not worry about paint—do not even give it a second thought. You will want to have all of your selections on your Big Details firm before you pick paint. Paint colors should be the last selections you make for your new home so that you can pull inspiration from the items in the rooms that you selected. So, happy news: no need to lose your sanity on paint selections . . . yet!

5

SELECTING A BUILDER—AND *THEN* A DESIGNER

Now that you have a firm rough idea (an oxymoron that works so well in this field) of the general direction of the style of your home, it is time to take a big leap and start to find your builder.

Rule Number One: Find your builder *before* your designer, and have him or her involved in the design process from the very first meeting. This will ensure that you have an extra, independent set of eyes on your plans so that nothing is missed. Often people will start with a designer for their plans, and then once completed they take them to their builder. They then discover that the plan is not only out of budget but has issues with regard to items like mechanical space and proper chases. Having the builder on board from the start allows him or her to make sure you are staying in line with

Quick Note:

A custom home is a personalized design just for you. A home from a production builder is generally offered from existing pre-designed floor plans with customizable options available.

Jargon Watch:

A construction document set is the entire set of drawings and details you need to build your home. Some projects may be a simple and only require drawings of the site plan, framing plan, floor plan, roof plan, elevation drawings, and electrical, while others will require very meticulous drawings making the construction document set to be well over fifty pages with details of everything from wall cross sections down to the finishes in a room.

regard to your desired budget. If you are not in budget it can be addressed *during* the design process. It is always most efficient and cost-effective to make your changes on paper early on in the process before you have a set of construction documents. Making drastic changes to your plans after you have a construction document set is not only costly, but it can affect you emotionally.

By the time you finish a plan, you become very attached to it and will find it very distressing to have to change it.

It is also very common that a builder will own the lot, and in order to build on that lot, you must use that builder, and that is the only option. This dynamic is unique from the standpoint that it is essentially a forced relationship, but I would suggest that you vet them the same way you would if he or she were not your only option.

GLIMPSE OF A CONSTRUCTION DOCUMENT

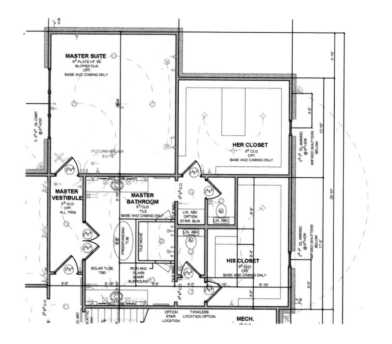

How to involve a builder before construction plans are drawn

BEFORE

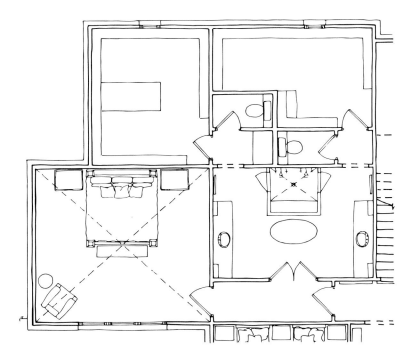

AFTER

Budget items to discuss with builder

+ Can we tile the wall in the master bath?

+ Put in a steam shower?

+ Add a chandelier to the master suite?

+ Run tile in master bathroom into vestibule and suite?

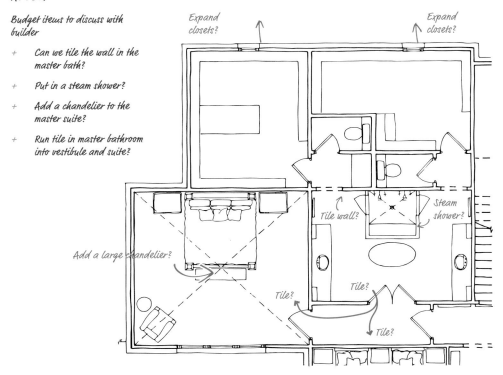

INTERVIEW YOUR BUILDER

It is imperative that you take the time to sit down with your potential builders and ask them many questions in order to get a read on how they work. When interviewing a builder here are some important questions to ask:

What were the costs per square foot of your most recent homes?

Have your most recent homes come in at or near the estimated budget?

Did your most recent homes reach completion at or near the estimated timeline?

Would you say that now is a good time to build?

How long have you been building in this area?

Do you have recommendations of draftsmen, designers, or architects you work well with?

Can we visit two or three past projects you have completed?

Can I have three references of past clients whose homes you have built?

CALL REFERENCES

Get at least three references of clients they have built for within the past five to ten years. I know it is awkward to call up perfect strangers and ask them what they thought about their builder, but suck it up and do it! You want to hear from past clients what they thought and any feedback they may have, both good and bad. The reason you want to try and get past clients from five years or more ago is so that you can inquire about the durability of their house and how the builder has addressed warranty items.

Here are some questions you might ask them.

BUILDER-CLIENT WORKSHEET

↘ CLIENT 1 ADDRESS

↘ CLIENT 2 ADDRESS

↘ CLIENT 3 ADDRESS

Have you been pleased with your home?

↘ CLIENT 1

CLIENT 2

CLIENT 3

Do you feel that your relationship with the builder was good throughout the construction process?

CLIENT 1

CLIENT 2

CLIENT 3

Did you come in at or near budget?

↘ CLIENT 1

↘ CLIENT 2

↘ CLIENT 3

Did you come in at or near the estimated timeline?

↘ CLIENT 1

↘ CLIENT 2

↘ CLIENT 3

How has the builder been with regard to taking care of warranty items?

↘ CLIENT 1

↘ CLIENT 2

↘ CLIENT 3

If you were building again, would you use the same builder?

↘ CLIENT 1

↘ CLIENT 2

↘ CLIENT 3

After you have interviewed two or three builders I would compare notes and then really just go with your gut. Building is stressful, and you want to make sure you really trust and like the person running the show.

WE HAVE A WINNER!

Enter all of your builder's information below.

BUILDER

CONTACT NUMBER

E-MAIL ADDRESS

FAX NUMBER

MAILING ADDRESS

NOTES ON YOUR BUILDER

SELECTING YOUR DESIGNER OR ARCHITECT

As I stated before, the first piece of the puzzle is to have the builder in place—but I also understand that every situation is different and every market is different. So whether you pick your designer or architect first or after your builder, here are questions to ask them.

INTERVIEW YOUR DESIGNER OR ARCHITECT

It is imperative that you take the time to sit down with your potential designer or architect and ask them lots of questions in order to get a read on how they work, and if they are a good option. When interviewing a designer or architect here are some important questions to ask.

How do you charge for plans?

What drawings are included in your construction document set?

How do you charge for changes to the plans?

What is the expected timeline to complete a set of plans?

[Best case scenario timeline]

[Worst case scenario timeline]

After we complete the plans, do you have the right to sell the plans to other people? If so, is there a mileage rule as to how near to my project?

How many meetings should I expect during the process and how often?

Do you draw preliminary furniture on your plans? (This is a must!)

If we have special pieces of furniture, can you draw them on the plans?

Do you have any past client references I can call on?

Do you have a good working relationship with any builders or contractors?

CALL REFERENCES

Just as with your builder, get at least three references from previous clients. Again, I *know* it is awkward to call up perfect strangers and ask them what they thought about their designer or architect—but suck it up and do it! You want to feel great about pushing forward with the person or firm that will be drawing up your dream home, so be armed with as much information as you can to make a good choice.

DESIGNER-CLIENT WORKSHEET

 CLIENT 1 ADDRESS

CLIENT 2 ADDRESS

CLIENT 3 ADDRESS

How did you feel about the design process?

CLIENT 1

↘ CLIENT 2

↘ CLIENT 3

Do you feel that your relationship with the designer was good throughout the entire design process?

↘ CLIENT 1

↘ CLIENT 2

↘ CLIENT 3

Did you come in at or near budget?

↘ CLIENT 1

↘ CLIENT 2

↘ CLIENT 3

Did you come in at or near the estimated timeline?

↘ CLIENT 1

↘ CLIENT 2

↘ CLIENT 3

Do you feel that they listened to your desires as well as your concerns?

↘ CLIENT 1

↘ CLIENT 2

↘ CLIENT 3

Were their preliminary furniture plans accurate with regard to space and flow?

↘ CLIENT 1

↘ CLIENT 2

↘ CLIENT 3

Did you run into any issues during construction that stemmed from the drawings?

↘ CLIENT 1

CLIENT 2

CLIENT 3

If you were building again, would you use the same designer?

CLIENT 1

CLIENT 2

CLIENT 3

YOUR DESIGNER OR ARCHITECT

Enter all of your designer or architect's information below.

DESIGNER OR ARCHITECT

CONTACT NUMBER

E-MAIL ADDRESS

FAX NUMBER

MAILING ADDRESS

6

STARTING THE PLANS

Things are really starting to fall into place now. You have your team selected and feel good about your decision! However, it is one thing to daydream about your future home and look at images and finishes you love, but it is entirely another process when it is time to put the pencil to the paper and start laying out the floor plan.

ROOM REQUIREMENTS

The first thing you will need to do is determine your needs with regard to rooms. Tick the rooms below that pertain to your plan and write the number required next to the rooms you have ticked.

☐ Bedroom (including master suite) ---------

☐ Full bathroom ---------

☐ Half bathroom ---------

☐ Garage ---------

☐ Foyer ---------

☐ Mud entry ---------

☐ Grocery entry ---------

☐ Kitchen ---------

☐ Pantry ---------

☐ Butler's pantry ---------

☐ Chef's pantry ---------

☐ Bulk pantry closet ---------

	Dining area—formal	- - - - - - - - -
	Dining area—casual	- - - - - - - - -
	Breakfast room	- - - - - - - - -
	Breakfast bar	- - - - - - - - -
	Living area—formal	- - - - - - - - -
	Living area—casual	- - - - - - - - -
	Den	- - - - - - - - -
	Men's den	- - - - - - - - -
	Theater	- - - - - - - - -
	Keeping room	- - - - - - - - -
	Game room	- - - - - - - - -
	Playroom	- - - - - - - - -
	Family room	- - - - - - - - -
	Great room	- - - - - - - - -
	Utility	- - - - - - - - -
	Craft room	- - - - - - - - -

- [ ] Study   - - - - - - - - -
- [ ] Office   - - - - - - - - -
- [ ] Office nook   - - - - - - - - -
- [ ] Library   - - - - - - - - -
- [ ] Music room   - - - - - - - - -
- [ ] Motor court   - - - - - - - - -
- [ ] Basement   - - - - - - - - -
- [ ] Hobby room   - - - - - - - - -
- [ ] Craft room   - - - - - - - - -
- [ ] Hidden room   - - - - - - - - -
- [ ] Safe room   - - - - - - - - -
- [ ] Balcony   - - - - - - - - -
- [ ] Sunroom   - - - - - - - - -
- [ ] Screen porch   - - - - - - - - -
- [ ] Outdoor living   - - - - - - - - -
- [ ] Chapel   - - - - - - - - -

☐ Gallery   ---------

☐ Stairwell   ---------

☐ Pool house   ---------

☐ Pool bathroom   ---------

☐ Detached apartment   ---------

☐ Attached apartment or in-law suite   ---------

☐ Shop   ---------

☐ Barn   ---------

☐ ----------------------------   ---------

☐ ----------------------------   ---------

☐ ----------------------------   ---------

☐ ----------------------------   ---------

☐ ----------------------------   ---------

☐ ----------------------------   ---------

☐ ----------------------------   ---------

☐ ----------------------------   ---------

SUMMARISE YOUR NEEDS

Write down all the rooms you have ticked.

REVIEW YOUR LIFESTYLE AND PLAN ACCORDINGLY

There are a few lifestyle issues that will play a big role in the design of your home. Some are listed on the next page, but due to the nature of life, we cannot list them all! Feel free to add your own. The list should get you thinking about how you live day-to-day and how your lifestyle needs to be addressed within your floor plan. Start to pay attention to how you live each day—how you bring in the groceries, where you drop your junk when you walk in the door, and the like. Think about these types of behaviors and how you can improve upon them compared to your current setup.

LIFESTYLE CONSIDERATIONS

Tick the sentences that sound like you.

HOW DO YOU EAT?

- [ ] You cook often and eat at home
- [ ] You do not cook often and mainly eat out

OCCUPANTS

- [ ] You have young children ----------
- [ ] You have teenage children ----------
- [ ] You have grown children ----------
- [ ] You have grandchildren ----------
- [ ] You have inside pets ----------
- [ ] Have an elderly parent or special needs person in the house ----------

DAILY ROUTINE

- [ ] You spend most of your time indoors
- [ ] You spend as much time outdoors as possible

ENTERTAINING

- [ ] You often entertain guests in a formal setting with a caterer
- [ ] You often entertain guests in a casual setting

☐ You often entertain guests outside

☐ You do not entertain guests often

How many people do you usually plan to seat? _____

☐ You often have overnight guests

HOUSEKEEPING & MAINTENANCE

☐ You do your own housekeeping

☐ You have a housekeeper

☐ You (or others) often enter the house muddy

☐ You tend to be a pack rat

☐ You tend to purge often

SPECIAL CONSIDERATIONS

☐ You work from home often

☐ You may need the AC units zoned well so when the entire house is not being used it can be turned off (or in energy saving mode). This can occur if you travel often or do not use your entire home daily.

☐ You have a collection of items that need to be displayed

DAILY HABITS

☐ You often come home with lots of stuff that needs places (e.g. cell phones, brief cases, backpacks, and the like)

☐ Your household usually watches separate TVs at the same time

☐ Your household is very much into TV

☐ Your household is not concerned with TV

☐ You enjoy burning fires in the fireplace

☐ You read often and need book storage

CYCLICAL NEEDS

☐ You decorate for all four seasons

☐ You have lots of Christmas decorations

☐ You have seasonal clothes to be stored

OTHER NEEDS

List any other needs you think your designer or architect would need to know about to design your building effectively.

DETERMINE YOUR SQUARE FOOTAGE

Architects and designers measure square footage using two methods. The first is *total covered square footage*. This square footage takes into account everything that is under your roof—both air-conditioned areas and non-air-conditioned areas. This is used up until the design phase, as the total covered square footage is not as significant (particularly cost-wise). Most plans and budgeting will be based on the other method—*total livable square footage,* which includes all areas that are heated and cooled. Before your initial meeting with your designer, have a rough idea of square footage (both total covered and livable), but remember: this is usually just an estimate and jumping-off point. Typically this number is calculated by the client's budget and worked backward. The best strategy is to start out with the smallest figure you are comfortable with, as plans have a tendency to increase in square footage as you work on them. If, for example, you are currently living in 2,000 square feet and you want to double your living space (and have the budget to do it), do not go into the designer's office with a goal of 4,000 square feet. Start with a goal of 3,700 square feet. This way, as you see the plan develop, you can easily add square footage to the areas that you desire as opposed to playing a game of trying to cut out square footage. It is much easier to add square footage then to take square footage away.

SQUARE FOOTAGE WORKSHEET

TOTAL COVERED SQUARE FOOTAGE
(This includes garages and porches.)

_____ feet squared.

TOTAL LIVABLE SQUARE FOOTAGE
(Your starting goal.)

_____ feet squared.

MAXIMUM SQUARE FOOTAGE
(The most you can build.)

_____ feet squared.

Once the plan is underway, you have begun the difficult task of visualizing reality by looking at a 2D plan. This is a difficult task for experts, let alone for everyday folks, when you do not deal with it on a regular basis. One way to get more accurate

Quick Tip:

Do not relive issues that are a feature of your current home. You have already lived in the spaces in your house and understand if they work well, so make those dimensions your sounding board.

///////////////////////////

measurements for your specific requirements on a floor plan is to measure and tape. Buy some painter's tape, and use it on your floor! Measure all of your current rooms to establish their dimensions, and compare all the new spaces on your floor plan to that. For example, if you have a 15-by-15-foot master bedroom that you feel it is the perfect size, and the master on your floor plan is 18 feet by 22 feet, save yourself the square footage. Take it out of the master and put it where you need it. On the flip, if your current master is 15 feet by 15 feet and is too small with your furniture, but your new floor plan shows your master to be 15 feet by 17 feet, then add square footage to your master. If this problem has been an issue in your current house, do not relive the issue. You have lived in the spaces in your house and understand if they are too big or too small. Make those dimensions your decision basis.

Use the painter's tape when you are trying to really get a feel for spaces that do not have a direct comparison in your current home. If you are not sure if the master bath-shower they have designed for you is big enough (or can hold two people at once), go into one of your larger rooms, and use the painter's tape to tape off the dimensions onto the floor that are marked on your floor plan. Once you are standing in the taped space, move around in it, and get another person to join you. If the shower is designed for two people, but three of you can comfortably fit and move around, you will know that that the space is big enough and maybe even too big.

Alternatively, if the shower is designed for two people and just you and one other person pretending to wash your hair hit elbows, then clearly the space is too small. It may sound like a cheesy exercise, but it is much better to take the time to do this as opposed to discovering the squeeze the first time you use your shower.

This method will give you a good perspective as to your designed spaces, and help you evaluate each room to determine if the size drawn is a good fit for you and your family.

MASTER PLAN

Do not underestimate the value of creating a master plan. It may be that right now all you can afford or have the sanity to do is the main house, but your dream down the road is to have a pool, pool house, workshop and mother-in-law suite. Whatever your personal dreams are for your property, be sure to address those items on the plan now. Having a master plan in place will help you to make better decisions as you grow older with your home. It can be heartbreaking to tear down perfectly well-constructed buildings because later down the road you decided you really did want that pool or barn, but you don't have enough room. Plan, plan, plan! Master planning not only pertains to your floor plans and site plans but also to the finishes on the inside and outside of the home. Very often, your dreams are bigger than your budget, but this is where good planning and lots of patience are essential. It may be that you really want hard wood floors in your master bedroom or granite for all countertops but only carpet and laminated countertops are in the budget. Don't get discouraged—set goals and develop a master plan to upgrade as you can afford it! The biggest goal is to not build yourself into a box that you feel stuck in and that the only way to escape is to bust out of it!

LONG TERM PLAN

Write down any items below that you would like to see in your dream master plan.

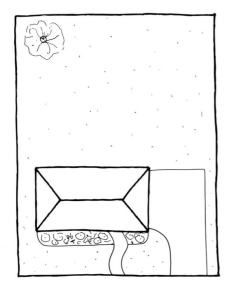

SORRY, NO CAN DO

It is just as important to establish your style preferences as the type of design you do *not* like. Take a bit of time to think about architectural elements that you are not keen on. Use your words, and tell your architect or designer, "I appreciate the suggestion, but that style is not for me." For example:

"I do not like dormers and shutters."
"Stucco and brightly colored doors make my skin crawl."
"I do not like brick, and copper creeps me out for some reason."

Whatever it may be, note it, and let your designer know.

NO-GO ITEM LIST

Items we/I **do not** like

THE IMPORTANCE OF FURNITURE ON PLANS

I have found that people often underestimate just how important furniture plans are. They think, "Oh, we will just figure it out when we move in," only to find when they move in that their china cabinet which has been a family heirloom does not fit in their new dining room—or against any other wall in the house for that matter. Yikes! Or they move in and realize that their living room has so many circulation paths through it that they cannot pass through the room without bumping into furniture. It is very hard to understand what in the world it means in terms of what furniture will fit and how much furniture will fit when you see that a room is a blank 16 by 18 feet. See the drawing below.

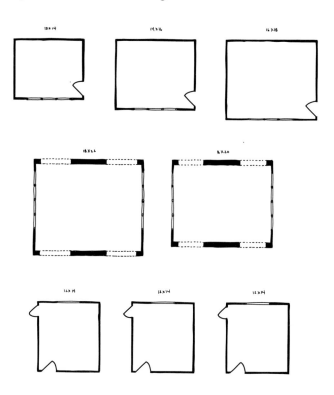

I am guessing when you look at these blank drawings of rooms you can understand a whole lot of nothing about them except where the doors are. Sure, a 12-by-14-foot is smaller than a 16-by-18-foot—but again, aside from knowing it is smaller, you probably understand a whole lot more of nothing about what furniture can fit in one room versus the other. So take those same blank rooms and add furniture like in the drawing below:

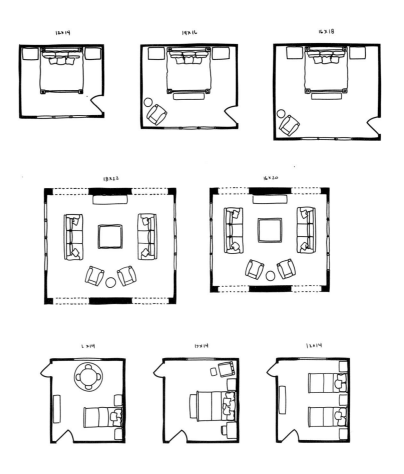

Suddenly, seeing the furniture drawn in, 12 by 14 feet and 16 by 18 feet DO mean a whole lot to you! You can right away see three different furniture layout options for a room that is 12 by 14 feet, or you can see that a 16 by 18 feet might be more room than you need for the king bed and night stand you plan on using. Or, in the 16-by-20-foot living room layout, you can see that when you walk in it you would be walking right into the side of the sofa and would have a tight squeeze around the back of it to pass through, but the same furniture layout with 18 by 22 feet creates a space behind the sofas that is comfortable to pass through when going through that room to get to the next room.

Of course, creating a furniture layout is not as easy as just dropping in a bed or a sofa. You need to take a lot of things into consideration to make sure that the furniture plan not only just works but works for how you plan to use the space. When conveying your needs to your designer it is important to have thought through what the function of the space will be and how many people will be using that space with regularity. For example, if you know that, a few times a month each month, you will be entertaining and serving dinner to a group of twelve to fifteen people, make sure that your furniture layout easily accommodates all twelve to fifteen people in the same room without the need to pull out a leaf on a table that then makes the table too big for the space, such that you then have to drag in chairs from other spaces to all cram around the table. If, on the other hand, you only entertain twelve to fifteen people once a year, and as a standard only need seating for six, then putting up a folding table or pulling the leaf out on the table for that one day out of 365 days in the year is a perfectly good option. So take advantage of the planning process now, and address these types of things early on in the design phase. Think through how many people you will need to seat in your living area, dining area, outdoor area, or how often you have out-of-town guests. Also consider how many beds you need to accommodate those guests if it will be a regular occurrence. You will also want to think through what pieces of furniture you plan to take with you, and give the dimensions of those pieces of furniture to your designer before they start to design your plans. I know there are good apps out there that can help you with your furniture placement once you know the dimensions of your room, and I think those are great to use when really fine-tuning the layout, but the first time you see a preliminary furniture plan needs to be on your preliminary floor plans. You cannot properly study a floor plan or determine your likes and dislikes without knowing how furniture will work in the space.

FURNITURE PLANS AND ELECTRICAL

The preliminary furniture plan is also a very important tool with determining the placement of your recessed lighting, lighting fixtures, and floor plugs. If the design of your room and furniture plan warrants that a chandelier hang exactly centered flanked symmetrically with recessed lighting and floor plugs directly under the sofas, this can then be conveyed on the floor plans so that when the concrete is being poured and the house is being framed the contractors will know that the floors plugs and lighting have specific locations that need to be addressed. This type of preplanning might seem demanding, but it is far less grueling to take the time to plan it out than to get on the construction site and realize that, due to framing, you either have to pay some expensive change orders to get your lights centered just right or live with off-centered lights and no floor plugs.

GOOD RULES OF THUMB ON FURNITURE PLAN SPACING

↘ Seating should be no farther apart than 8 to 10 feet in areas meant for chatting.

↘ In rooms where there will be a lot of pass-through traffic, allow a minimum of 36 to 48 inches of space uninterrupted by any furniture piece for the heavily trafficked route.

↘ Aim to have your main circulation spaces go around your furnished areas, not through them.

↘ The walking space around a dining table should be a minimum of 48 inches on each side and there should be at least 6 to 8 inches of space between chairs.

↘ The walking space around a bed should be a minimum of 30 inches.

↘ Take into consideration items like wall vents and floor registers when laying out your furniture so that you do not risk covering them up and making them less efficient.

SUMMARY PAGE FOR YOUR DESIGNER

Congratulations on making it to this point! Phew! You have had to ponder lots of things to get here, so go celebrate and eat some cake!

Fill out the information to the right to give to your designer before you start your plans.

 DESIGN SUMMARY

LOT INFORMATION

GOAL SQUARE FOOTAGE

MAX SQUARE FOOTAGE

ROOM NEEDS

EXTERIOR STYLE

INTERIOR STYLE

EXTERIOR VERTICAL MATERIALS

ROOF

FRONT DOOR

WINDOWS

GARAGE DOORS

EXTERIOR JEWELRY

LANDSCAPE

LIFESTYLE MAIN POINTS

ITEMS THAT ARE DISLIKED

ITEMS TO ADDRESS WITH YOUR BUILDER

As you get more in depth on your plans, you are going to want to start asking your builder some questions on the home construction and process—and you want to feel comfortable with the answers.

MORE BUILDER QUESTIONS

What type of foundation are you planning on doing?

(Examples include slab-on-grade and pier-and-beam.)

Will there be preplanned drainage around the slab and if so, what kind?

What type of vapor barrier will you use on the foundation?

Will you be pretreating the foundation for termites?

What type of framing will you use? (Examples include 2-by-4, 2-by-6, aluminum stud, and block.)

When will you start my sample wall?

What type of insulation do you generally use? Are you familiar with foam?

What types of pipes do you use for plumbing and why?

Do you use conduit in walls, attics, and under concrete for easy future expansion of things such as electrical and cable?

When will you give me my building allowances?

How do you charge for changes during construction?

What is the best method to use to convey concerns to you during construction?

What are the names of the stores/wholesalers that you generally work with when selecting your roof, exterior material, plumbing, appliances, floorings (tile, wood, and carpet), backsplashes, countertops, etc?

When you get the answers from the builders it is important to ask "why" these things are used as a standard. For example, in West Texas the standard for plumbing has become poly (which has replaced copper pipes), as the water in West Texas is extremely corrosive. If you were not aware of the reason behind this decision you may be very uncomfortable to see your slab poured and plumbing being roughed in with material you are not familiar with. Your knee-jerk reaction may be to think that the builder is cutting corners, when the reality is that he is doing what is best for your home.

CONDUIT

Let's take a minute to talk about conduit (which is generally a long tube made of PVC but can be made of other materials as well). Conduit is one of those decisions that seems insignificant until it is time to use it—and then suddenly it is a superhero! Run conduit in as many places as possible. It will save the day. For example, some clients think that they don't care about lighting their trees. They move into their home and then realize that the neighbors all celebrate the festivities by lighting up their house like a Christmas tree. They change their minds and want to get in on the action. Without having run conduit, they would have had to get special equipment to burrow under driveways and sidewalks while dodging other utilities that have been laid in the ground. This can be a timely and costly endeavor unless you have preplaced conduit. If you have planned to have conduit there, all you have to do is locate it under your driveways and sidewalks, and fish the line through. Bam! Crisis averted! Another example is when clients think they do not want cable for TV or internet in certain rooms, but once they move in they realize that they use the spaces slightly differently than they anticipated. They now want it on the second floor in an awkward spot—and all of the walls are covered up and insulated. Enter conduit that was laid between the first and second floors for future wiring to save the day! Suddenly something that would otherwise be a major headache becomes a very minor issue.

Here are some places that I suggest to run conduit. Tick any you may wish to notify your builder of.

- [ ] Under the driveway. If the driveway is large, run several.
- [ ] Under flowerbed edging.
- [ ] In tight attics
- [ ] Above true cathedral ceilings
- [ ] Between floors

If you live in an area with highly corrosive water, it is good to create **conduit sleeves** for your plumbing so that if you have a leak in your pipes you do not have to bust out your foundation to repair it. You simply pull the pipe from the conduit sleeve and replace the pipe.

7

THE "BIG DETAILS"

As you are working on finalizing your plans, you will need to start wrapping your hands around the "Big Details." This will also help your builder to give you the most accurate pricing and your architect information of things that need to be addressed on the plans—such as ceiling heights and treatments and wall treatments . At this stage of the game, you do not need to have firm and locked-down selections, but you need to start getting in the ballpark of the types of finishes and fixtures that you like. The builder will set the budget with given allowances for your project based on the types of materials you desire for your new home. If you are unsure of what a building allowance is, here is a good way to think about it. For example, as children, many people received a certain amount of money each day or week for lunch called a lunch allowance. If your parents gave you $25 for lunch that week, and you decided to go mad in the cafeteria and spend

$18 on day one of that week by buying lots of bags of chips and soda for you and your friends, then you were going to have a long and hungry week with only $7 left to spend. This is the same thing with your building allowance. If your builder has given you an $8 per square foot of tile allowance for the project (based off of your initial selections you provided) and you knowingly select a tile that is $12 per square foot, then this project is on a dangerous trajectory of busting the budget if you do not immediately lower the allowance in another area.

If budget is not a concern for you, then go for it, pick what you want, but be warned that things add up fast. Most people, however, regardless of if they are building a $150,000 home or a $4,000,000 home, will have allowances that they need to work within to stay on budget. It is very easy when you are making the interior selections of the home to have eyes that are bigger than your wallet. You must remember that every Big Detail has a range of price tags just like cars do. There are economic compact cars, midsize sedans, and top-of-the-line luxury vehicles. Do not walk onto the car lot and test drive the Ferrari if all you can afford is a minivan. Do yourself a favor: walk into the store (tile store, granite store, plumbing store, whatever it may be) and ask to be shown the items you are looking at in your specific price range and put on blinders to everything else. It is easy to want the top of the line of everything when you are out shopping, but if you end up getting entranced with each Big Detail, then you can kiss your budget good-bye and say hello to a truckload of stress.

Once you have made your preliminary selections for the Big Details and have a preliminary floor plan, your builder will be able to give you initial pricing that will direct you as you finalize your floor plans.

Here is an example to illustrate how much the Big Details can drastically determine the direction of your selections based on budget, even if the layout of the rooms and appearance of the space on a floor plan is identical.

SCENARIO 1

You select hand-scraped, wide-plank wood floors, smooth texture walls, aluminum-clad windows, compound crown molding, 10-inch base board, with a wainscot of painted shaker panels and solid stained Alder doors. The cost of this room would be in the range of $16,000 to $20,000 to complete per those specifications.

SCENARIO 2

You select midrange carpet, spray texture walls, vinyl windows, no crown molding, 6-inch base board, and hollow-core paint grade doors. The cost of this room would be in the range of $6,000 to $8,000 to complete.

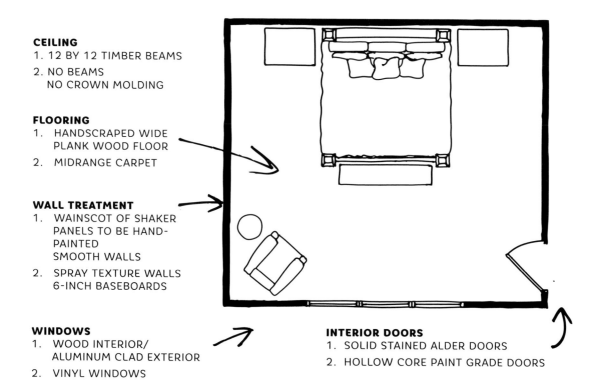

CEILING
1. 12 BY 12 TIMBER BEAMS
2. NO BEAMS
   NO CROWN MOLDING

FLOORING
1. HANDSCRAPED WIDE
   PLANK WOOD FLOOR
2. MIDRANGE CARPET

WALL TREATMENT
1. WAINSCOT OF SHAKER
   PANELS TO BE HAND-
   PAINTED
   SMOOTH WALLS
2. SPRAY TEXTURE WALLS
   6-INCH BASEBOARDS

WINDOWS
1. WOOD INTERIOR/
   ALUMINUM CLAD EXTERIOR
2. VINYL WINDOWS

INTERIOR DOORS
1. SOLID STAINED ALDER DOORS
2. HOLLOW CORE PAINT GRADE DOORS

The Big Details are very important in determining cost of your home, as you can see that both Scenario 1 and Scenario 2 had the exact same square footage and footprint but the costs are drastically different.

STAY ORGANIZED

Staying organized when making your selections of the Big Details is also key to a successful building experience. The sister app to this book will help you to organize your potential selections as well as lock in your final ones. All too often, people make a selection on an item and then they forget or cannot find the information on the item as they go to make their next selection. You want to make sure that as you make selections you build upon each one based off of the previous selection you have made. If you are unorganized, this can be very hard to do and you end up with a final product that looks more piecemeal than planned.

DECISIONS, DECISIONS, DECISIONS

Remember, regardless of whether you hire a professional designer or not, you will have to make *lots* of decisions in this process—there is no way around it. Most people are not aware just *how many* decisions you have to make during the process, so be prepared. Each time you make one decision, know that there is another decision right around the corner. By being mindful of this, you will set your expectations properly and you will not find yourself frustrated thinking, "If I have to think about one more thing for this house, I am going to lose my mind." Hopefully, you will see it coming and not let it discourage you, because you know at the end of the tunnel is a big light called a finished house! Hang in there!

ABOUT THE BIG DETAILS

Previously (on the biggies list), you made your selections and prioritized them. The exact opposite is true for the "Big Details." You need to prioritize right out of the gates in order to set your expectations correctly and make good decisions. Keep in mind that this list may evolve as you begin to research your options, but you must remember that if something becomes the new most important thing, then something needs to become the least important. Recall, this is often where clients get into trouble with the budget.

Take time to list your Big Details on page 152, and put them in priority order. Number one is the most important and number fifteen is the least important.

→ Appliances

→ Built-ins

→ Ceiling treatments

→ Countertops

→ Flooring

→ Hardware

→ Interior doors

→ Light fixtures

→ Plumbing fixtures

→ Texture

→ Trim

→ Backsplashes

→ Glass and mirrors

→ Wall treatments

→ Window treatments

YOUR BIG DETAILS PRIORITIZED BY BUDGET

1
- -

2
- -

3
- -

4
- -

5
- -

6
- -

7
- -

8
- -

9
- -

10
- -

11
- -

12
- -

13
- -

14
- -

15
- -

Just as with the biggies, the dollar signs may not really be an exact indication of how much you will spend on each item. It is a visual to help you figure out in your head the items you are willing to splurge on as opposed to the items you are not so willing to bust open the bank for.

Once you have determined your list, share it with your builder so your allowances can be set accordingly.

If you are really not sure of what order things fall in for you, here is a good suggested priority order. This order is based off of what item is the hardest to upgrade at a later date verses what is easiest. Again, this is where master planning comes into play as discussed under "Master Plan" on page 119.

Number one is the most important (hardest to change) and number fifteen is the least important (easiest to change).

Keep in mind that just because something is the easiest to change does not mean that it is the cheapest. The ease of upgrading down the road is based on the idea that if you are already living in the home, what items would be the least disruptive to your day-to-day life as you are upgrading, and what things would you literally have to move out of the house to get accomplished.

We can rank these with stress faces as per the next page.

STRESS INHERENT IN THE BIGGIES

→ Flooring ☹☹☹☹☹☹☹☹☹☹☹☹☹☹☹

→ Backsplashes ☹☹☹☹☹☹☹☹☹☹☹☹☹☹

→ Appliances ☹☹☹☹☹☹☹☹☹☹☹☹☹

→ Texture ☹☹☹☹☹☹☹☹☹☹☹☹

→ Ceiling treatments ☹☹☹☹☹☹☹☹☹☹☹

→ Wall treatments ☹☹☹☹☹☹☹☹☹☹

→ Built-ins ☹☹☹☹☹☹☹☹☹

→ Trim ☹☹☹☹☹☹☹☹

→ Countertops ☹☹☹☹☹☹☹

→ Plumbing fixtures ☹☹☹☹☹☹

→ Light fixtures ☹☹☹☹☹

→ Interior doors ☹☹☹☹

→ Window treatments ☹☹☹

→ Glass and mirrors ☹☹

→ Hardware ☹

GETTING SAMPLES IS A MUST

In making selections, one of the most important tasks you have to do is to get samples. Take a Sharpie to label all the information about them as soon as you get them.

A good place to start with making selections is with flooring. You would start with going to the flooring store. While you are at the store, narrow your flooring options for each room down to your top two (or if you can pick your top one then seize the moment and run with it—way to be decisive!). You will be doing this for each room in your house. It may turn out that you have only one type of flooring for the entire house, or it may be that you want a different flooring in almost each room. Whatever floats your boat; just be sure and snap a picture of your selection, file it away on the app, and request a sample that you can keep. On the back of the sample write down how much the sample costs per square foot, what the lead time is on that material and what brand that material is (if that information is not already on it). Once you have those samples they will be your constant companion for the process.

Once you have your flooring samples in place, the next step would be to take those samples as you select your countertops. Once you determine your countertops (and have taken pictures of them and filed them away in your app), you will take the samples of your flooring and countertop with you to make the selection for your backsplashes. You will continue to collect your samples and build upon them with each step as you work your way through all of your

People will often wait to start doing their preliminary selections on all of these Big Details until floor plans are finished—that is a huge mistake. You don't want to have completed plans and realize as you are making selections that you are now in love with interior doors with transoms or timber-beamed ceilings, but it will take major onsite changes to now incorporate them—this usually equates to more time and more dollars.

\\\\\\\\\\\\\\\\\\\\\\\\\\\

Big Details selections. You will continue this process until your last selection is made. You will want to purchase a cheap roller suitcase to store all of these samples in to make sure they do not get lost—and to make it easy to take the samples from store to store with you. There will be times when it will not be practical to have all of the samples with you, which is why having your app up-to-date with all samples is imperative. Also be sure to view all of the samples you get multiple times during the day so you can see how the colors change. They will be affected by morning light, afternoon light, and evening light, as well as artificial light at night.

As you are working through your final decisions, here is a good rule of thumb to help you create a timeless look that you will not soon tire of. Go neutral with your flooring, countertops, and backsplashes in your main areas. In those areas, add bold pops of color and character on things that are easy to change, such as furniture, accessories, and lighting. If you want to do something fun and more trendy and timeless, do it in an area that you use often, like the powder bath or utility room, so you can enjoy it but where it will not become a polarizing issue when you go to sell the house.

The next few pages will take each Big Detail and discuss it briefly. The Big Details will be discussed in the suggested order that they should be picked based on the most logical order to make the selections—not based off the priority given to it with regard to budget.

Use the Simpleigh Done app to organize your decisions. ↗

FLOORING

There is a vast array of flooring options on the market today. When considering your options the biggest thing to think about is your lifestyle. If you have a big, light-colored dog that tends to shed, or you live in a dusty desert, a solid-colored dark floor would be a maintenance nightmare. If you have long, dark locks that you like to style daily, you will want to avoid putting white or very light colored flooring in your bathroom. As you are looking for flooring materials, think about what type of foot traffic will be on them (pets, grown people or kids). Will you be cooking over those floors or

walking in with muddy feet? You want to balance durability
and functionality with appearance.

Here are common flooring options:

- Bamboo
- Carpet
- Cork
- Laminate
- Linoleum
- Stained concrete
- Tile (real stone, ceramic, or porcelain)
- Wood (engineered)
- Wood (real)

Your most expensive floors are generally wood and real
stone tile—but they add great value to your home, as well
as a timeless aesthetic quality. Your least expensive floors are
generally carpet (although there are a few amazing break-
the-bank carpets), linoleum or laminate, but they are not as
durable, do not age as well, and are not seen to add value to
your home. Stained concrete, cork, bamboo, porcelain tile,
and ceramic tile fall in the middle range with regard to cost
(but can also creep up in cost depending on what type and
brand you select), and their durability and longevity varies.
If installed correctly, concrete can have an aesthetic and
durability that is hard to beat. However, if stained concrete is

installed poorly, it will serve as an oversized eyesore. Note that is it always helpful to take a look at work the flooring installer has recently completed to ensure that their quality is good, but with concrete it is imperative. With stained concrete, visit two or three old projects to ensure their quality is consistent.

Very often people think, "Phew—check my flooring off the list!" when they have selected their flooring material, only to show up on site and have the flooring installer ask questions like:

What size of wood plank or tile?

What pattern do you want it laid in?

What direction do you want the pattern laid?

What type of sealer do you want applied to it: matte or glossy?

Then they are on the site and must come up with an answer to these questions that they are rushed in making and really not all that sure about. The key here is to process these questions immediately after you have made your flooring selection so that you are prepared and confident in your decisions. Reviewing these questions in advance will allow you time to study pictures of the flooring you like in your inspirational images, and visit flooring showrooms or example floors to hone in on what you want so you know the answers before you are asked on the day.

Now refer back to the inspirational images you have gathered, and try to focus on nothing but the flooring. After looking at floors, do you still feel like the style in the inspirational image is a good fit for you? Take pictures of all of the flooring samples you have narrowed down, and file them in your app. You will want to review these images with your builder so they can let you know if you are in line with the initial budget you have discussed.

COUNTERTOPS

Just as with flooring, when selecting your countertops be prepared that the options are vast and your lifestyle should dictate your selections. Each type of countertop has its pros and cons. No countertop comes without some considerations and maintenance requirements.

Here is a list of the most common options for your countertop:

- Concrete
- Corian
- Butcher block/wood

↘ Glass

↘ Granite

↘ Laminate

↘ Limestone/travertine

↘ Marble

↘ Quartz

↘ Soapstone

↘ Stainless steel

↘ Tile (real stone, ceramic, or porcelain)

PROS AND CONS

Floors may have a lot of foot traffic but countertops have a lot of *everything* traffic.

They get items tossed on them, things spilled on them, food prepared on them, and really hot things put on them, so it is important to think about the pros and cons of countertops as you are making the decisions for each of the rooms in your house.

CONCRETE

Pros

Durable, heat resistant, infinitely customizable, and can be seamless.

Cons

Expensive, and can crack if not sealed correctly annually. It is susceptible to staining—especially from oils.

CORIAN

Pros

Easy to repair when damaged, wide range of colors and styles, and can be seamless.

Cons

Not heat resistant, not stain resistant, can easily scratch, and is sensitive to chemicals.

BUTCHER BLOCK/WOOD

Pros

Easy to repair when damaged, can be sanded down and completely refinished, gentle on dinnerware, and can get more beautiful with age.

Cons

Easy to scratch and dent, not heat resistant, if not sealed or oiled correctly annually will be susceptible to swelling from water, easily stains, and can harbor bacteria if used as a cutting board.

GLASS

Pros

Very stain resistant, very hygenic due to its nonporous surface, and durable if over 1 inch thick.

Cons

Expensive, can chip and crack, cannot be repaired if damaged, not heat resistant, and shows fingerprints easily.

GRANITE

Pros

Highly durable, heat resistant, stain resistant if sealed properly, holds up to chemicals, wide range of colors and styles, each slab is unique, and has a very long lifespan.

Cons

Expensive, not easy to repair if damaged, should be resealed every few years.

LAMINATE

Pros

Cost effective, stain resistant, low maintenance, and comes in a wide range of colors and styles.

Cons

Not heat resistant, can crack, is hard to repair, and does not age well.

LIMESTONE/TRAVERTINE

Pros

Generally more cost effective than granite, heat resistant, and has a long lifespan.

Cons

Easy to scratch, can trap food and bacteria if its pits are not sealed, susceptible to staining, sensitive to chemicals, and should be resealed annually.

MARBLE

Pros

Heat resistant, long lifespan, and can get more beautiful with age.

Cons

Expensive, not easy to repair if damaged, susceptible to staining, sensitive to chemicals, and should be resealed annually.

QUARTZ

Pros

Highly durable, scratch and stain resistant, no sealing required, holds up to chemicals, and is virtually maintenance-free.

Cons

Expensive, not easy to repair if damaged, and not heat resistant.

SOAPSTONE

Pros

Heat resistant, stain resistant, holds up to chemicals, is very hygienic, and its appearance can be altered by oiling it.

Cons

Expensive, easy to scratch and chip, and high maintenance if you decide to oil it.

STAINLESS STEEL

Pros

Stain proof, holds up to chemicals, and is very hygienic, as it inhibits bacterial growth.

Cons

Expensive, easy to scratch, is noisy, and shows fingerprints easily.

TILE

Pros

Can be cost effective, durable, easy to repair if damaged, easy to install, and is generally heat resistant (some materials more than others).

Cons

Uneven surfaces and grout lines can easily get stained.

 # GRANITE WORKSHEET

Circle any granite edges below that appeal to you.

STANDARD EDGES

SQUARE	¼" ROUND	EASED	BULLNOSE	DEMI BULLNOSE
BEVEL	MEDIUM BEVEL	DEEP BEVEL	COVE	OGEE
COVE OGEE	DUPONT	COVE DUPONT	REVERSE BEVEL	CHISELED

LAMINATED EDGES

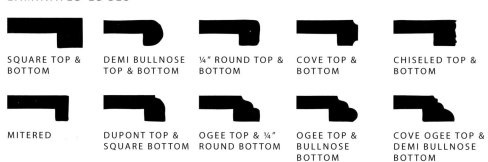

SQUARE TOP & BOTTOM	DEMI BULLNOSE TOP & BOTTOM	¼" ROUND TOP & BOTTOM	COVE TOP & BOTTOM	CHISELED TOP & BOTTOM
MITERED	DUPONT TOP & SQUARE BOTTOM	OGEE TOP & ¼" ROUND BOTTOM	OGEE TOP & BULLNOSE BOTTOM	COVE OGEE TOP & DEMI BULLNOSE BOTTOM

Now refer back to the inspirational images you have gathered, and try and focus on nothing but the countertops. After looking at countertop options, do you still feel like the style in the inspirational image is a good fit for you? Take pictures of all of the countertop samples you have narrowed down, and file them in your app. You will want to review these images with your builder so they can let you know if you are in line with the initial budget you have discussed.

APPLIANCES

Appliances are tricky nowadays because they just do not make them like they used to—where they would run forever, and fixing them was a simple process.

When making your selection on appliances you will want to think about how often you will be using them. If you are not an intense cook or aspiring chef, kitchen appliances are a place you can really save money or upgrade down the road. However, if you are a whiz in the kitchen or just have a joy for cooking, then give yourself a generous budget to get top-of-

//////////////////////

Quick Tip:

Feedback on online product reviews can be misleading. People often purchase appliances based on online customer reviews only to have a long road of nothing but trouble from this supposed top-rated appliance.

The best research you can do to gather proper intel on appliances is to call your local appliance repair person and quiz him or her. Ask them to tell you what brand of appliances have had the most problems. Ask them what their experience has been like with customer service and warranty items for the brands they deal with. This should give you solid feedback on what appliance brands might be your best bet.

\\\\\\\\\\\\\\\\\\\\

the-line appliances. There are some spectacular appliances on the market that will make daily life in your kitchen a wonderful experience!

Another big decision you will want to make is if you want all of your appliances to be exposed or if you want to have some appliances like the refrigerators and dishwashers fully integrated (meaning fully concealed in the cabinets). There is a big difference in aesthetic between fully integrated and exposed, as well as a wide array of prices for both, so be sure and take the time to study the difference of the two. Here is a list of large appliances to consider for the home inside and out.

+ Range (built-in)

+ Range (freestanding)

+ Cooktop

+ Vent hood

+ Oven (single)

+ Ovens (double)

Quick Tip:

Do not stick with just one dishwasher or one washer and dryer because that is what is typical. If you entertain often and have a large kitchen, go with two dishwashers and an oversized refrigerator and freezer with spare refrigeration in the pantry. If you have a big family, plan for space for two washers and two dryers. Having two appliances like described above will greatly improve your quality of life.

+ Microwave (built-in)

+ Microwave (drawer)

+ Microwave (countertop)

+ Warming drawer

+ Ice maker

+ Coffee maker (built-in)

+ Dishwasher (full)

+ Dishwasher (drawer)

+ Refrigerator/freezer combination

+ Refrigerator (full)

+ Refrigerator (drawers)

+ Freezer (full)

+ Freezer (drawers) ☐

+ Wine refrigerator ☐

+ Beverage refrigerator ☐

+ 24-inch refrigerator ☐

+ Trash compactor ☐

+ Washer ☐

+ Dryer ☐

+ Washer/dryer combination ☐

+ Grill (freestanding) ☐

+ Grill (built-in) ☐

+ Smoker ☐

A NOTE ON SMALL APPLIANCES

Often small appliances are overlooked until you move in and realize, "Oh darn, my mixer and countertop coffee machines are too big to fit in my cabinets, and I use them all the time, so I'll just set them on the counter." Wham! All of a sudden, your countertop has now been sacrificed to small appliances. When reviewing the layout of your kitchen be sure to think about the location of all of these appliances. If you use some appliances daily like a toaster, blender or coffee maker, look into incorporating an appliance garage into your design. This is a great way to keep them handy but have them tucked away when not in use.

Now refer back to the inspirational images you have gathered, and try and focus on nothing but the appliances. After looking at appliance options, do you still feel like the style in the inspirational image is a good fit for you? Take pictures of all of your appliance options you have narrowed down, and file them in your app. You will want to review these images with your builder so they can let you know if you are in line with the initial budget you have discussed.

BACKSPLASHES

A backsplash is frequently where people think it is best to get a little crazy and fun and spend a little extra on making it a focal point. This logic can sometimes work, but it rarely results in timeless appearance. As stated earlier, go neutral with the backsplashes in your main areas such as the kitchen and master bathroom. In those areas add bold pops of color and character on things that are easy to change such as furniture, accessories and lighting. I'll say it again—if you want to do something fun and more trendy and timeless, do it in an area that you use often, like the powder bath or utility room, so you can enjoy it but where it will not become a polarizing issue when you go to sell the house.

Keep this in mind—neutral does not mean boring and colorless. It can still be exciting and have color, just not bright blue with pink polka dots. You can still have patterns, but use tone-on-tone patterns, or a subtle color en masse. You want the backsplash to be a piece of a beautiful picture—but not to dominate the entire visual.

Tile is more often than not the backsplash of choice. Here is a list of common types of backsplash tile:

+ *Ceramic tile*   ☐

+ *Glass tile*   ☐

+ *Porcelain tile*   ☐

+ *Metal tile*   ☐

+ *Natural stone tile*   ☐

Here is a list of other materials that can also make great backsplashes:

- ✚ Brick (thin or whole) ☐
- ✚ Chalkboard paint ☐
- ✚ Copper ☐
- ✚ Cork board ☐
- ✚ Granite ☐
- ✚ Limestone/travertine ☐
- ✚ Marble ☐
- ✚ Magnet board ☐
- ✚ Stainless steel ☐
- ✚ Stone ☐
- ✚ Wallpaper ☐
- ✚ Wood (plank or panel) ☐

Backsplashes are one place that you will probably acquire more samples for than any other part of your house. Once you have made some preliminary selections, take the samples you have and put them in the areas you are thinking of using them. For example, if you are thinking about using a glass tile in your kitchen for the backsplash, tape it up in your existing kitchen and live with it. Looking at a sample in the environment you intend to use it in for a few days in a row will help you to determine what materials you are crazy about and what ones you can eliminate. Also, if you are leaning toward something different from the norm, like chalkboard paint or a magnet board in a place like a kitchen or bathroom, get a sample board of it, set it behind the sink, and take note of how it holds up to water being splashed on it and food being flung on it.

Do not overthink or pull your hair out over your backsplashes (this is a common occurrence after visiting the tile store or kitchen showroom)—it is easy to be overwhelmed by the endless amounts of options you have before you. If all else fails, pick one nice material and go with that, keeping in mind that it is a nice backdrop for all of the other things going in your kitchen.

Now refer back to the inspirational images you have gathered, and try and focus on nothing but backsplashes. After looking at backsplash options, do you still feel like the style in the inspirational image is a good fit for you? Take pictures of all of your backsplash samples you have narrowed down, and file them in your app. You will want to review these images with your builder so they can let you know if you are in line with the initial budget you have discussed.

BUILT-INS

A built-in in a home is generally defined as an item such as a cabinet or shelf that is constructed to be a permanent part of the home. A good rule of thumb with built-ins is less is more. There are areas such as the kitchen, utility/laundry, and closets that built-ins without question are the only feasible and best option. Other places they tend to be a good options for are designated studies or libraries. Areas that have great options for both standard built-ins or furniture are bathrooms. It adds instant personality to a bathroom to transform an old piece of furniture into a vanity, or even purchase some of the furniture vanities that can now be found in all of the major home improvement stores. In areas such as bedrooms, dining rooms, living rooms, garages, craftrooms and the like, furniture is a better investment to make to address storage needs, and it often will add better character to the space. Furniture is always more versatile, and is an investment that you can take with you in the event you have to move or change the way in which you use a space. *Do not let the idea of resale rule you— but always be mindful of it.* An empty room with no built-ins can be a nursery, guest bedroom, craft area, office, or men's den. The role of that empty room is simply determined by the furniture you put in it. But what if you were to take that empty room, for example, and add built-ins to make it a designated home office. A year later you discover you are now expecting a new little miracle to the family, and that designated office must now become a nursery. You must now painfully rip out those built-ins that you spent so much money on to make the room functional for your current needs. There are some situations where the shape and function of a room is so unique that a piece of furniture cannot work. In these situations ask yourself, "Is the built-in I am constructing going to not only solve the problem of storage in this room now and for the next fifteen years—as well as solve the exact same problem the next homeowners would have if I have to move?" If the answer is yes, I would push forward on the built-in. If the answer is no, solve the problem the best you can using furnishing—or simply give away some of your stuff. It is pretty common to create a whole lot of storage for a whole lot of things that you never really use. It may be hard but often the best solution to solving your storage needs is not always better designed storage but rather generously giving away the things you do not need. A move into a new home is a perfect time to tackle that challenge.

NOT JUST LOTS OF STORAGE— BUT GOOD STORAGE

The key to having good storage in your built-ins is not always accomplished by simply have lots of it. Being smart with how you design your storage and lay out your spaces is the key to victory. When you are searching inspirational images take note of some of the specialized storage methods available such as vertical pull-outs, spice drawers, pull-out shelves, lazy susans, appliance garages, appliance lifts, cabinet pull-down shelves, canned goods shelves, pull-out tables and cutting boards, vertical cutting boards and cookie sheet slots, and trash can drawers.

TAKE AN INVENTORY

Not fun. It is time-consuming. But very worth it.

Take note of how you will be using each space and what tasks you are wanting to accomplish. In the kitchen, if you are a great baker you will want to make sure your kitchen design supports the task of baking with proper storage for your ingredients as well as necessary appliances. In the utility/laundry, if you are a whiz with the iron and ironing board, make sure the design addresses their location. A big mistake people make is to design their spaces without actually taking stock of their needs. They just assume that they will make the storage work when they move in only to realize that their stuff does not fit in their new house! The best way to avoid this is to take your plans and actually label on them where you items will go.

This may not end up being exact, but it will at least get you in the ballpark and help you have your storage needs at the forefront of your mind. The two most important places to take inventory of what you have and what your specific storage needs are is the kitchen (including your pantry) and master closet. If you do not have the time or patience to do every room, do those two. As you are taking inventory of what you have, also take note of the things that you like and dislike about the current storage in your house. Then make sure you are not repeating any of these mistakes in your new house. Don't try to take stock of all of your needs in one day, because you will overload your brain and get overcome by it all. Breaking things down and doing no more than one room in a day (or even just one part of the kitchen) is a good planned pace. Use your app to document the likes and dislikes you currently have, as well as needs you have for your built-in storage. Document pictures of the type of storage you like in your app.

The hard part of built-ins is determining what in the heck kind of storage goes in them—but the fun part is what they look like!

Here are common questions to think about for your built-ins:

↘ *Are they going to be stained or painted?*

↘ *What style of cabinet door and drawer do you want?*

↘ *Are they going to be inset or overlay?*

↘ *Will they use finger pulls or hardware?*

↘ *Will they be self-closing or have full extension tracks?*

↘ *Will your hood be an exposed appliance or a decorative built-in with a hidden element?*

Insist on seeing cabinet drawings before you sign off on any cabinet design. These drawings will help you visualize what you have been looking at in 2D on your floor plans as well as make it easier to verify that all of your storage needs are met. Once you have your built-in drawings, take the floor plan drawings that you labeled your storage needs on, and transfer those labels onto the built-in elevation drawings. This will confirm that you have proper places for all of the items that will need a special spot in your new home.

Example Plan of a Kitchen Built-In with Storage Outline.

1. OVERSIZED PLATTERS
   GLASS PUNCH BOWLS

2. FORMAL GLASSES
   AND BOWLS

3. CASUAL GLASSES

4. SEASONAL PLATTERS
   AND DECOR

5. PLATES AND BOWLS

6. OILS AND SPICES

7. MIXING BOWLS

8. GLASS STORAGE
   CONTAINERS

9. DISH SOAP

10. CLEANING BUCKET

11. EATING UTENSILS

12. UTENSILS

13. DISHCLOTHS

14. TABLECLOTHS

15. BAKING
    SHEETS

1. OVERSIZED PLATTERS
   GLASS PUNCH BOWLS (HIGH)

2. FORMAL GLASSES
   AND BOWLS

3. CASUAL GLASSES

4. SEASONAL STORAGE
   (HIGH)

5. PLATES AND BOWLS

6. OILS AND SPICES

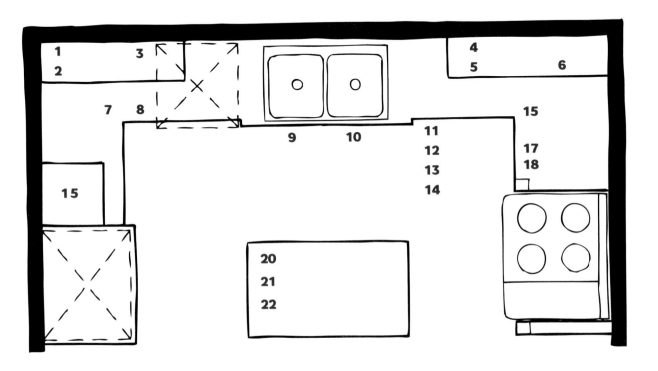

7. MIXING BOWLS

8. GLASS STORAGE
   CONTAINERS

9. DISH SOAP

10. CLEANING BUCKET

11. EATING UTENSILS

12. UTENSILS

13. DISHCLOTHS

14. TABLECLOTHS

15. APPLIANCE GARAGE

16. BAKING SHEETS

17. COOKING UTENSILS

18. OVEN MITTS

20. CHIP CLIPS

21. ZIP LOCK STORAGE

22. BARBECUE TOOLS

Now refer back to the inspirational images you have gathered, and try and focus on nothing but the built-ins. After thinking about your built-in needs, do you still feel like the style in the inspirational image is a good fit for you? Take notes about all of your built-in needs and styles you are leaning toward, snap pictures of your built-in drawings, and file them in your app. You will want to review these images with your builder so they can let you know if you are in line with the initial budget you have discussed.

TRIM

Trim is one of those subtle items that has a big impact on evoking specific style to a room. A carved compound crown molding with door surrounds that have appliques may set a tone for a highly formalized and traditional home, whereas a very square and clean line crown molding and base will evoke a more contemporary feel. In prioritizing trim, it is best to put the most budget into the base and door casing because they are almost always in your line of sight, especially when you have tall ceilings (see graphic on page overleaf).

Line of Sight when looking at trims.

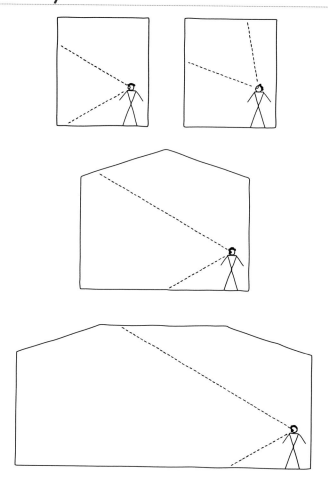

Trim Terms to Consider

- » Crown molding
- » Cap
- » Door casing
- » Door jamb
- » Door header
- » Window casing

- » Window jambs
- » Window header
- » Window sill
- » Baseboard
- » Plynth blocks

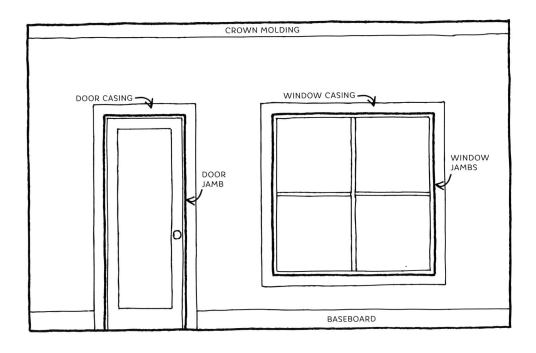

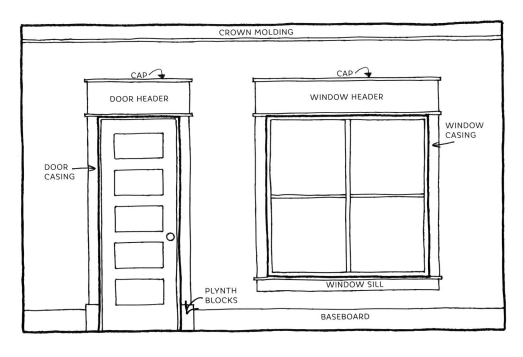

Now refer back to the inspirational images you have gathered, and try and focus on nothing but the trim. After thinking about your trim, do you still feel like the style in the inspirational image is a good fit for you? Note the type of baseboard, crown molding, door casing, and window casing in your app that you like. You will want to review these images with your builder and trim carpenter so they can let you know if you are in budget and so you can give them clear direction on what to do.

INTERIOR DOORS

There are three common types of doors: hollow core (a very lightweight paint-grade door that has a cardboard-like or foam center and is very cost-effective), solid core doors (a durable paint-grade door that mimics the feel of a real wood door), and solid wood doors.

Hollow core doors generally cost around $40, solid core doors generally cost between $80 and $120, and solid wood doors vary in cost greatly depending on the type of wood they are. They can cost as little as $200 a door to well over $1000 a door.

It is always surprising how quickly doors can add up. An average three-bedroom, two-bathroom home may have as few as ten interior doors or as many as fifteen or more, depending on the floor plan. A five-bedroom, three-bathroom home may have as few as twenty interior doors or as many as thirty-five or more depending on the floor plan.

See the chart below to see how quickly interior doors can become a large expense based on the three- and five-bedroom examples discussed above:

DOORS	HOLLOW	SOLID	WOOD
10	$400	$800-$1,200	$2,000-$10,000
15	$600	$1,200-$1,800	$3,000-$15,000
20	$800	$1,600-$2,400	$4,000-$20,000
35	$1400	$2,800-$4,200	$7,000-$35,000

Unlike other Big Details, the selection of an interior door can be very straightforward in the same way selecting a garage door can be. Sure, there are still decisions to be made and items to choose from, but they are not as endless as when you are dealing with items like backsplashes and countertops.

The style of doors on the market varies, but there are a few safe roads to take and some to never travel down.

The first road you want to travel down is the solid core road or solid wood door road. If you see the road for the hollow core door, do NOT take that exit. It may be tempting to cut costs here and go with hollow core doors, but only do that if you have full intention of upgrading your doors in the near future. Hollow core doors are not sturdy, do not create a good sound barrier, and do not age well. A solid core door or solid wood door will always be your best bet.

If you took the solid core door road your next stop should be Smooth Lane. Avoid Texture Road. Do not even look down Texture Road—bad things happen down that road.

If you select a solid core door, go with a *smooth* texture. A smooth texture exudes a high-end and more authentic look then a textured one. A textured door demonstrates a low-end and dated look.

If you took the solid wood door road, your next stop is Samplesville.

If you go with a solid wood door, request a piece of wood the door is made from so that you can test out stain samples

////////////////////////////

Door Tip:

Not all of the doors in your home have to match. Do not be afraid to do some great barn door sliders, glass French doors, decorative metal doors, etc., to highlight certain areas of the home such as a study, pantry, great room, etc.

\\\\\\\\\\\\\\\\\\\\\\\\\\\\\

////////////////////////////

Firm Tip:

Select a solid core or solid wood door.

\\\\\\\\\\\\\\\\\\\\\\\\\\\\\

before applying stain to your doors, as well as add them to your collection of samples for the house you have gathered.

You are almost to your destination when you make it to Pick-Your-Style Boulevard. This Boulevard has many tempting turns to make, and the one turn you *do not want to make* is Arch-Top Panel Street. If you see that Street, drive away as fast as you can, and do not look back.

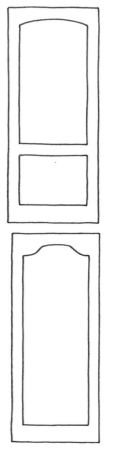

As you are picking your styles there are a few to avoid. Arch-top panels like the ones in the two images on the side will either compete with the nice arched cased opening that you may have in your home, or they will be the only arched thing in your home and just will not make sense.

If an arch is a design detail in your home, pick a few key doors and make them arched. A handful of truly arched doors will prove to be much more sophisticated than just an arch-top panel on all of your doors. Alternatively, you can take a square door and add an arched transom.

If you really are indifferent or just cannot decide on what type of door to go with, both of the styles to the right are great options. They have a timeless appeal and really are a chameleon of style. They take on the nature of the casing trim around them.

ABOVE Arch-top no-nos

Door Tip:

The door trim and door do not have to match. Do not be afraid to paint your door casing and stain your door!

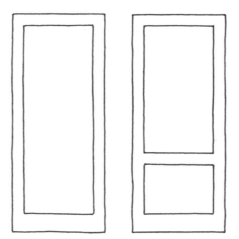

ABOVE Great door options

INTERIOR DOOR OPTIONS

Use the sketches below to get thinking about the type of interior doors that you will use. Circle any that interest you.

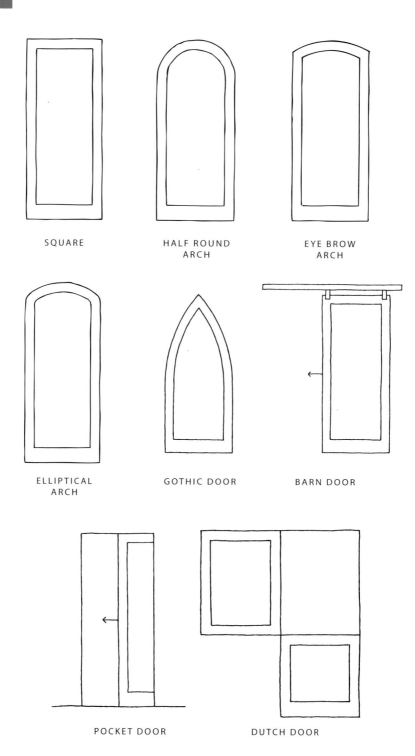

SQUARE

HALF ROUND ARCH

EYE BROW ARCH

ELLIPTICAL ARCH

GOTHIC DOOR

BARN DOOR

POCKET DOOR

DUTCH DOOR

INTERIOR DOOR WORKING OPTIONS (DOUBLE)

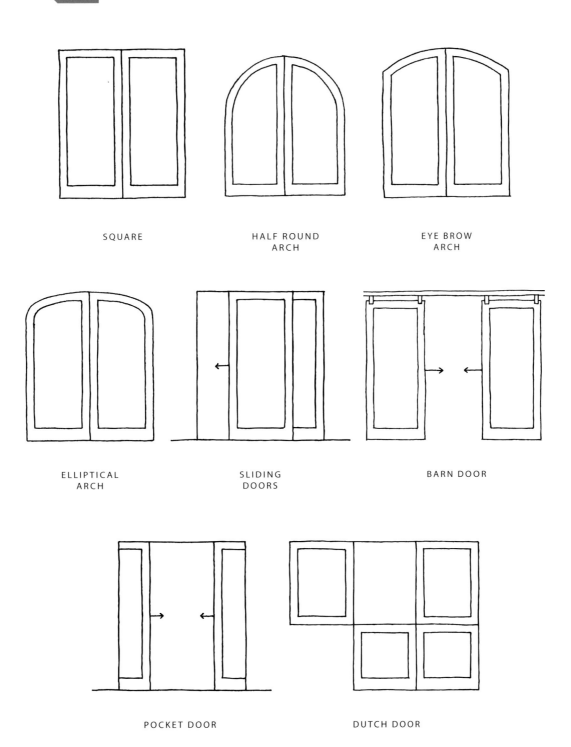

SQUARE

HALF ROUND
ARCH

EYE BROW
ARCH

ELLIPTICAL
ARCH

SLIDING
DOORS

BARN DOOR

POCKET DOOR

DUTCH DOOR

Door Tip:

Think about what will stop your door from banging a wall when it opens. A good option is a small door stop that installs on the hinges. Traditional door stops tend to get damaged and kicked off the wall or break toes, but a hinge stop helps you to avoid both of those pitfalls.

Now refer back to the inspirational images you have gathered, and try and focus on nothing but the doors. After thinking about your interior doors, do you still feel like the style in the inspirational image is a good fit for you? Note the type of door (wood, painted, arch-top, or square), and put the ones you like in your app. You will want to review these images with your builder so they can let you know if you are in line with the initial budget you have discussed.

CEILING TREATMENTS

One of the first factors to consider when determining your ceilings is scale. Your goal should be to enhance a room by adding excitement to the ceiling and not making it unpleasant to be in.

A good rule of thumb is the larger the space, the taller the ceiling, and the smaller the space, the lower the ceiling. A change in ceiling heights can also help to create a differentiation between public and private spaces. If you walk from a bedroom with a 9-foot ceiling into a games room with a 12-foot ceiling, you will have a clear sense that you are now in a public space.

A ceiling height carries as much impact in a room as a light fixture or the tile on the floor. People often get hung up on the idea of high ceilings everywhere, but that frequently has the same effect as if you were to have the exact same chandelier in each room. The first time you saw it, it would be exciting, but after the third or fourth time you saw it, it would just become commonplace. It is also often overlooked that all of that volume you are adding to the house has to also be heated and cooled. If you get too carried away with high ceilings, you will literally be paying for it each month in the form of your utility bills.

Determining ceiling heights is one thing, but trying to figure out what ceilings to embellish is another. Some styles, such as *rustic* and *Mediterranean,* lend themselves toward high ceilings with dramatic additions such as timber beams or painted murals. Other styles, such as *craftsman* and *shabby-chic,* will lend themselves toward more moderate ceiling heights with simplistic treatments such as wood plank or boxed-out beams. The style you have selected for your home will very much dictate what type of ceiling treatments will enrich the spaces. If your budget is big, you may have ceiling treatments in over half of the rooms of your house. If your budget is on the lower end, you may only have one or two treatments, and if this is the case, focus those treatments in areas where you will spend the most time. People are repeatedly drawn into doing very tall entry foyers and will put their money in that tall ceiling, but this is not a good decision. The foyer is generally a quick pass-through, and in order to enjoy the ceiling, you have to cock your head back and stop walking. You are better served to focus your initial budget for ceiling treatments in the areas you spend the most time (such as the kitchen, living, or dining) and where the ceiling will fall into your line of sight more often than not. Once you address the ceilings in those high traffic areas, move onto areas such as entry rotundas and bedrooms if you desire more ceiling treatments.

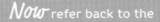

Now refer back to the inspirational images you have gathered, and try and focus on nothing but the ceiling treatments. After thinking about your ceiling treatments, do you still feel like the style in the inspirational image is a good fit for you? Note the type of ceiling treatments you are leaning toward and the location for those treatments in your app. You will want to review these images with your builder so they can let you know if you are in line with the initial budget you have discussed.

WALL TREATMENTS

Wall treatments vary greatly not only with regard to style but also with purpose. A wall of tile might look great but also be there because it is in a mud room that gets filthy and needs to be a surface that can easily be cleaned. You might add chalk paint to a wall because you want to direct your child's artwork to it and away from your pristine, smooth white walls. All function aside, you might add fabric panels or a painted

Quick Tip:

A powder bathroom is a great place to spend money on wall treatments (and ceiling treatments as well). This is one place where your guest, and even you, on occasion, will take a moment to literally just sit and enjoy all of the details of the room (if you know what I mean!).

\\\\\\\\\\\\\\\\\\\\\\\\\\\\\\

mural to a wall for no other reason than you think they look awesome. Whether the wall treatment is functional or purely aesthetic, your goal should be the same—to enhance the depth of character to a room with its addition. There are countless types of wall treatments—painted patterns, wood planking, wood paneling, tile cladding, brick cladding, wall papering and more—to explore, and they range from items you can easily DIY on a budget, to costly choices that require a professional to install. A wall treatment does not always have to encompass the entire wall. Some treatments can overwhelm a space if there is too much of it. When you are considering a wall treatment, visualize the treatment at a chair rail height (about 36 inches), at a wainscot height (about 32 to 54 inches), and at a three-quarter wall height (generally 72 inches and up, depending on ceiling height). Thinking about the treatment at each one of these heights will help you to determine just how much of that treatment you need. Not all walls are always alike either. There are times when it makes sense to have all four walls with a treatment and others when it makes sense to have only one wall with an embellishment. Thinking about the potential treatment on one wall, two walls, three walls, or all four walls will help you to determine the best location for it. When prioritizing wall treatments, start with the ones that you genuinely need to help control the wear and tear of your home and if there is anything left in the budget after that, work out from there!

Now refer back to the inspirational images you have gathered, and try and focus on nothing but the wall treatments. After thinking about your wall treatments, do you still feel like the style in the inspirational image is a good fit for you? Note the type of wall treatments you are leaning toward, and note the height and location for those treatments in your app. You will want to review these images with your builder so they can let you know if you are in line with the initial budget you have discussed.

PLUMBING

Before you begin to determine if your kitchen faucet will work
by no more than a touch or if your master shower will be the
residential equivalent of Niagara Falls, you will want to do your
homework on what will actually be coming out of the faucet:
the water. The quality of water in the area you are building
could have a big impact on what brand of plumbing fixtures
you go with. Some waters are so heavy with minerals that they

can build up quickly and wreak havoc on plumbing fixtures. If you are a lucky one and are building in an area where the water out of your tap could just as soon be bottled, the world of plumbing is your oyster. The best way to determine if the quality of your water is an issue or if you should be brand specific when selecting your plumbing fixtures is by calling two or three local plumbers. Ask them for feedback on local water quality and if they have experienced bad luck with any specific brands and good luck with others. Once you are armed with this information, you can push forward with making your selections.

Note here what you have learned from the local plumbers.

The first place to start with plumbing fixtures is to select your sinks, bathtubs, and toilets. These selections will help you to better select complementing faucets and showerheads. If you are initially attracted to a highly contemporary freestanding bathtub, that will not only guide you to a complementary style of faucet but also require a very specific type of faucet that you will have to choose from. Another example would be if you decide to go with a vessel sink for a bathroom that sits on the counter. Wall-mounted faucets are commonly selected to accompany these sinks, and they would require you to select a specific type of wall-mounted faucet. The same will be true with sinks and toilets. These fixtures will not only dictate things like faucets but the rough-in plumbing itself. If you are going to do plumbing that is not standard, the plumbers will need it brought to their attention even if it is already noted on the construction documents. You will not need your selections in the rough-in stage, but you will need a general idea of where you will have things like freestanding tubs, vessel sinks, and body sprays.

You could write a book on nothing but selecting plumbing fixtures due to the fact that there is such a vast selection with regard to both styles and finishes. Sinks can be stainless steel, cast iron in a range of colors, copper, glass, and hand painted, just to name a few, and the same could be said for bathtubs. Plumbing is an area that is easy to get disorganized and forget what you have selected or easily overlooked when making selections. Take the space below to review your plans in detail, and note all plumbing fixtures that you will need to make decisions on. Once you have your list, be sure and transfer all of your information and any pictures of your selections to your app.

List your plumbing needs here.

Here is a list of common plumbing fixtures to refer to when identifying your needs:

- Bathtubs (drop in and free standing)
- Bathtub faucets
- Body sprays
- Bidets
- Drain covers
- Sinks (kitchen, utility, and bathroom)
- Sink faucets (kitchen, utility, and bathroom)
- R.O. faucets
- Showerheads (wall mounted, ceiling mounted, and handheld)
- Toilets
- Urinals

A SIDE NOTES ON SINKS

Sinks come in four main forms:

Drop-in, which means there is a lip where the sink meets the countertop. The sink rests on top of the counter, and it is generally your most economic choice.

Under-mount, which means it is installed underneath the countertop and has no lip. The lack of lip makes these sinks easier to clean, but it also makes them more costly than a drop-in sink.

Vessel, which means it is a bowl that sits directly on top of the countertop. These are generally the most expensive sink options.

Pedestal, which means it is freestanding and requires no vanity.

A SIDE NOTE ON TOILETS

There are some beautifully designed and eye-catching toilets out there that come with tons of bells and whistles. But buyer beware, these awesome toilets often come with a headache for how often they malfunction. If you want one of these discussion-piece toilets, limit it to an area such as a powder bath and go with toilets that have a proven track record in the bathrooms you will be using daily.

A SIDE NOTE ON DRAINS

Some areas will have codes that may make it difficult to use some drains so it will be important to discuss this with you builder before you make your drain selections. Drains are often the most overlooked fixture when making plumbing selections. A great drain will deliver not only on function but on style as well. A unique drain can transform an otherwise ordinary shower.

A SIDE NOTE ON FINISHES

The most common finishes on the market today are brass, copper, chrome, oil-rubbed bronze, satin nickel, and stainless steel. It is easy to feel like your plumbing fixtures in the house must all match in finish, but that is not always the case. One thing to do is to take special note of which finish is the flush lever for the toilet. If all of your bathrooms do not have the same finish on the plumbing, be sure and match the toilet lever to the plumbing fixtures in each bathroom.

Now refer back to your inspiration images, and focus on nothing but the plumbing fixtures. After thinking about your plumbing, do you still feel like the style in the inspirational image is a good fit for you? Note the type of plumbing you are leaning toward, and note it in your app. You will want to review these images with your builder so they can let you know if you are in line with the initial budget you have discussed.

LIGHT FIXTURES

A light fixture in a room is like the cherry on the top of an ice-cream sundae. The sundae can still look appetizing, but it will never really look complete without the cherry on top. You can take a very neutral and unexciting space and add a spectacular chandelier, and voilà: you no longer have an unexciting space but now a room worth talking about!

The main forms of lighting are going to be integrated (meaning lights built into the wall, crown mold or cabinetry of the home), recessed cans, track, pendants, ceiling mounted, and wall mounted.

The sheer amount of light fixtures available today can even overwhelm the professionals when they are making selections. The most common styles of lighting today are art glass, contemporary, French country, industrial, mission/ craftsman, modern, old-world, retro, rustic, traditional, transitional, and vintage, and the finishes available in those styles are too broad to even begin to name.

The best way to get aquainted with which style of light fits you best is to search each style on Houzz.com and take note of the styles that appeal to you.

Note below your preferred styles—as well as your decorative-lighting needs in your home.

A SIDE NOTE ON LIGHTING FINISHES

It is tempting to want to make your lighting fixture finishes always match the finishes that you have selected for your plumbing hardware but do not get stuck in that rut. You want your finishes to coordinate but not to replicate.

Also, if you are building a traditional home, for example, do not feel that all of your lighting must be traditional as well. Doing this will make your home feel like it is one note. Explore the idea of adding a punch to a room by making the style of your decorative lights different than the general style of the home. See the example picture previously of a farmhouse with contemporary chandeliers.

A SIDE NOTE ON FANS

All too often, fans will get center stage in a room because that is all that people have been familiar with. There are awesome corner fans on the market today that allow you to have the best of both worlds: a fan and a chandelier. There are also exciting fans on the market today as well, so if a fan is going to get top billing in a room, make it count.

Now refer back to your inspiration images, and focus on nothing but the lighting fixtures. After thinking about and researching your lighting, do you still feel like the style in the inspirational image is a good fit for you? Note the type of lighting fixtures you are leaning toward and note it in your app. You will want to review these images with your builder so they can let you know if you are in line with the initial budget you have discussed.

TEXTURE

Wall texture may not sound like a big decision, but boy is it. The right texture can make a room feel inviting and the style complete—or the wrong texture can make a room feel off and out of step. Texture is also one of those things that once you have it up it is a major headache to change (from both the mess and the expense it would cause). Texture is often very driven by the style of the home. A smooth, very flat wall texture is the perfect match to a modern space, where as a heavier hand-troweled texture is a great fit for a rustic space.

Something that I have run into with texture that is very unique is that the expense of the kind that you want is largely dependent on what area you live in. In certain parts of the States, flat texture is the standard and most economical, but in other parts, it is far from standard and is very expensive.

There are lots of textures out there, but I feel that there are really only three good options.

SMOOTH TEXTURE

Pros

Smooth texture is the king of all textures. It has such a wonderful timeless quality and is a great fit for almost all styles. It really creates a tone is a room that is unmatched.

Cons

It can be expensive, depending on in what part of the US you are building, and if the drywall was not installed perfectly level, flat texture will not hide the flaws

HAND-TROWEL TEXTURE

Pros

Hand-trowel texture can really finish off the feel of a room in certain styles of home such as rustic and Mediterranean. It can also really hide flaws that might be present in the drywall.

Cons

The success of the aesthetic of a hand-troweled drywall is very dependent on the person who is doing the work. It is imperative with this type of texture that the person or persons applying the texture provide samples so that you can verify their work. It can also be expensive, depending on in what part of the US you are building.

SPRAY TEXTURE WITH HEAVY DRAG

Pros

Spray textures are the most economical and take the least amount of time. A spray texture with a heavy drag is a great middle ground between a smooth and hand-troweled texture. It can also really hide flaws that might be present in the drywall.

Cons

The aesthetic of a spray texture is inferior to the other textures and does not evoke the same level of timelessness.

Now refer back to the inspirational images you have gathered, and try and focus on nothing but the texture. After looking at these textures, do you still feel like the style of texture in the pictures is a good fit for you? Take pictures of the texture options you like, and file them in your app. You will want to review these images with your builder so that they can let you know if you are in line with the initial budget you have discussed.

GLASS AND MIRRORS

In general, your selections for glass and mirrors during
the construction process will be for your bathrooms. The
interior design of other rooms might incorporate mirrors, but
right now you need to only focus on the mirrors that affect
construction. The style and size of a mirror and type of shower
glass door you select for your bathrooms will have a major
effect on the overall success of the space.

MIRRORS

Mirrors are wonderful additions to a bathroom because they can make the room feel large and help bounce natural light around to make the room feel brighter. The amount of styles, sizes, and price ranges for mirrors is hard to even grasp; it is vast! The downside of this is that you can get overwhelmed with just how much there is to choose from, but the upside is that with enough looking you will likely find just the perfect mirror for just the perfect price.

Similar to light fixtures, you can take a very neutral and unexciting space and add a spectacular mirror and the bathroom that was once blah is now something to show off. As a general rule, if the bathroom is very ornate I would add balance to the space with a simple mirror, but if the space is very simple I would add excitement to the space with a sensational mirror! In most all situations, unless it is a very unique situation that calls for a mirrored wall or ceiling, I advocate using framed mirrors that hang on the wall. Having hanging mirrors gives you a lot of flexibility with regard to the style and finish as well as making it very easy to change the mirror out if you grow tired of it at some point. Do not be afraid to step out beyond your comfort zone on mirrors. Since hanging mirrors are an item that can be so easily changed, be brave! I often see that people will tend to want to match the mirror to the plumbing or to the vanity, but do not get caught in this trap. Do not think about matching the finishes in the room or making it match the vanity; make the mirror its own special self! But do not make it so unique that it does not serve its purpose. The mirror should be fabulous but also be functional. When you are selecting your mirrors be sure and ponder on how you will use them and ask yourself if the mirror you are picking will serve that purpose well.

Finally, if your bathroom storage space is tight, be sure and look into medicine cabinet mirrors. There are some really great ones on the market that will not only add character to the room but much-needed storage space too!

GLASS

One of the biggest things to consider when selecting the type and amount of glass you will use for your for showers will be the water quality where you live. Other factors you will want to consider when making your selections are budget, how private you like to be when showering (will you feel too exposed in a clear glass surround?), and whether you will be comfortable with the idea of your shower being seen by all when it is full of your shampoos and razors, etc.

There are two main types of shower doors—**frameless** and **framed**.

There are numerous options for glass, but here are four good options: **clear**, **frosted**, **textured** and **colored**.

Frameless clear glass showers are always my top choice because they make a space feel larger and make the shower an art piece. The only time frameless clear glass is not the most superior option is if you have lots of mineral buildup in your water. If that is the case, you then have to decide just how much you love frameless clear glass because you will have to squeegee it after every shower or spend a large chunk of change on special finishes that repel soap scum and mineral buildup to avoid the mineral buildup etching the glass. Daily squeegeeing is the only option with hard water to maintain the classic crystal-clear glass look. If you cannot maintain a crystal-clear glass, do not use it, because an etched shower surround with scum buildup is not an attractive look. You would be better off with a closed-in tile shower or tub/shower combo with a shower curtain. However, if you live in a place with really nice, pure water, then celebrate by using clear glass surrounds!

Although frameless clear glass surrounds are by far my favorite option, there are still other great options for your shower glass doors. In the past, framed showers were enclosed in a cheap, awful-looking silver or brass that notoriously would pull away from the glass and fall apart. They were cost effective and looked cost effective. The great news is that today there are some beautiful framed shower surrounds in dark aluminums and chrome that will make you turn your head and snap a picture of it!

If frameless clear glass doors/surrounds or high-end aluminum or chrome framed doors/surrounds are not options due to privacy concerns or budget, I would encourage you to go simple with the tile inside the shower and use a frosted, textured, or colored glass door and put your money and design focus into the other areas of the bathroom (lighting, cabinets, floor tile, mirrors).

People tend to want to do over-the-top tile in all showers, and when the glass is clear, I agree that this can be a great option. However, if you cannot see into the shower or bath except for the short time that you are in the shower (and usually, your eyes are shut, and water is running over your face), you will not really get to enjoy all of the expense that went into making that intricate tile happen. Conversely, if you know that down the road you want to have a clear glass surround but it is not an option with your current budget—go for the intricate tile now, and when you swap out the economical glass choice down the road, you will be able to bask in the once-hidden shower that will be beautifully displayed!

Now refer back to your inspiration images, and focus on nothing but the glass and mirrors. After thinking about and researching them, do you still feel like the style in the inspirational image is a good fit for you? Note the type of glass and mirrors you are leaning toward, and note it in your app. You will want to review these selections with your builder so they can let you know if you are in line with the budget you have discussed.

HARDWARE

One of the best things about hardware is that you have lots of time to ponder on it because it is one of the very last items to be installed in your home. Although it is important to consider other finishes in the space you are selecting hardware, like with lighting fixtures, do not get hung up on that. You want to strive to make finishes complement one another, not necessarily always match. Do not be afraid to mix things up with hardware, because they are easily changed if you tire of them. And hardware might be small and generally one of the last selections you make, but it has a big impact in the final appeal of a room, often referred to as the jewelry to your cabinets and doors.

The types of hardware available range greatly from inexpensive plastics to solid metals. The cost on them varies just as much as the material. It can be tempting to purchase inexpensive plastic hardware, especially at the end of the project when you have grown exhausted from spending money; however, with cheap hardware, you most certainly get what you pay for. With regular use, cheap hardware does not wear well and will generally lose its finish and start to fall apart. Your best bet is to go with a cost-effective solid-metal option.

It is important to keep in mind that you will be touching and handling your hardware daily, so you will want to purchase samples of the hardware you are interested in so that you can handle them and process the pros and cons of them. People have discovered many pitfalls of hardware by living with their samples. For example, people have taken home their samples and placed them up against a cabinet only to realize that the pull they selected is not actually wide enough for their hand to fit through or the knob that they were considering is too hard to comfortably grip. Taking your samples and simply replacing a piece of hardware already installed in your house takes only a matter of minutes, but it is those few minutes that will prevent you from a big headache down the road.

Just as you should not shy away from mixing finishes within the same space, do not shy away from mixing up knobs and pulls in some spaces as well.

Scale is also very important to take into consideration when selecting hardware. If you are making a selection for an area that has high ceilings and tall cabinets, a small knob will look strange and out of place, whereas a long pull might be the perfect fit for the space.

A SIDE NOTE ON HARDWARE

Just like with interior doors, the cost of hardware can add up fast. An average kitchen can easily have thirty to forty pieces of hardware, and if you find a perfect piece of hardware that is only $10 apiece, you might think, "It is only $10, why not go for it?" You would be right that $10 is a great price if all that you needed were one piece of hardware, but keep in mind that $10 times forty pieces of hardware is $400! Then think about the fact that each one of your interior doors needs hinges and door knobs, as well as all of the bathroom cabinets, etc., and not to mention the towel holders, hooks, and toilet paper holders. Pace yourself, and be mindful of your hardware allowance when making these selections. Lean on the builder to give you an idea of how much money you can spend on each piece of hardware and stay in budget.

Here is a list of the following pieces of hardware you will need to select:

↘ Cabinets

↘ Door stops

↘ Front door

↘ Hinges (doors and cabinets)

↘ Interior doors

↘ Secondary exterior doors

↘ Towel bars and rings

↘ Toilet paper holders

↘ Wall hooks

Note below your preferred hardware styles—as well as your needs.

Quick Tip:

There are two main types of door hardware: a door knob and a lever. If you will have young children in the home, keep in mind that a door knob is easier to baby proof on exterior doors, and levers are easier for a child to use to open doors.

Now refer back to your inspiration images, and focus on nothing but the hardware. After thinking about and researching hardware, do you still feel like the style in the inspirational image is a good fit for you? Note the type of hardware you are leaning toward, and note it in your app. You will want to review these selections with your builder so they can let you know if you are in line with the budget you have discussed.

WINDOW TREATMENTS

By the time you get to selecting your window treatments, you will probably have suffered lots of sticker shock along the way, but you will be very close to the finish line or may have even passed the finish line and already be living in the home.

Window treatments are really in a category of their own on cost. Pricing out window treatments is very much like ordering refreshments at a movie theater. You are already pretty taken aback by the cost to just buy your ticket, and when you go and order a soda or some popcorn and they tell you that it will cost you a million dollars—you might even say out loud, "Are you serious?!" Yep; prepare yourself, and maybe even sit down when you start to get prices back for window treatments, because you just might pass out.

Here are common options for window treatments:

- Plantation shutter
- Drapery
- Roll shade (electric and manual)
- Pull shade

Window treatments are a very important part of your home. It is one of the few items that will literally affect the look of your home from both inside and outside. When picking your treatments, always think about what they will look like from the street as well. One of the biggest mistakes that people make is to pick really bold draperies that, from the inside of each room, look great, but from the street, suddenly your house looks a bit like a color wheel or circus tent. Review your selections, and make sure that from the street there is great flow and consistency from window to window.

Window treatments also serve an important role in controlling privacy as well as natural light in a room. Good window treatments should also help to keep a room cool in the summer and warm in the winter, in turn helping with your utility bills.

When making your selections, be sure and also explore the ability for that treatment to serve as a blackout shade. Generally, an option to black out a room is important for those who enjoy a nap or those who have young children that sleep better when they cannot see that the sun is still up outside. Blackout shades can also have the biggest impact on your utility bills in the summer.

Now refer back to your inspiration images, and focus on nothing but the window treatments. After thinking about and researching window treatments, do you still feel like the style in the inspirational image is a good fit for you? Note the type of window treatment you are leaning toward, and note it in your app. Some builders will have an allowance built into the budget, and others will not. Be sure and discuss this with your builder.

Your "Big Details" list is crucial, as it forms the heart of the home. Your home is where you will live day in and day out, and the character that it will radiate stems from these selections. As you explore each Big Detail and refer back to your inspirational images, you may find your taste has changed as mentioned in the previous chapter. Be sure and swap out and update your inspirational images as you work your way through your selections.

So it is time to start using the app and getting your options and top picks in order!

8

CONSTRUCTION BEGINS

So the big day finally arrives—it is time to break ground!
Congratulations! Who knew that watching dirt be moved
could be captivating (or cost so much money)!

Breathe.

Take a deep breath. Construction is a highly stressful process
but so rewarding as well. If, during this process, you start to
get overwhelmed and frustrated, remember that the end goal
is a wonderful new home and all of the blessings that go
with that!

A few things to keep in mind:

1. Slabs always look deceivingly small so do not panic when you see your foundation—the house actually gets bigger with each step of the process. So when you go see and walk on your new foundation and feel yourself freaking out, reread this, and take a deep breath. If you determined the square footage of your house based off my suggestions on page 115 and took the time to really follow through with it, then you are fine.

2. Take care of the workers. Be polite and show gratitude. Bring the workers cookies or other treats. Show them you care. I feel that the more they feel appreciated the more they will strive to do good work on your home.

3. False expectations are the biggest root of disappointments, so prepare yourself to expect delays, things to not work out just as planned, and give some cushion to your deadlines in order to minimize stress during the process.

4. One of the hardest parts of the building process is to stay organized, so be sure and use the app to stay on top of your selections!

9
PAINT

Sometimes, the hardest part of a race is the last mile—but it can also be the most important. Picking paint really is the last mile of the race when building a home, and moving your furniture into your new home is like your trophy for the completion of the race. Even in writing this book, I have put off writing about paint until last. So this will not be the last chapter you will read, but believe me, it was the last chapter that I wrote!

It takes years for people to learn about colors and how they affect not only a room but the people in the room. The effects of paint color on you psychologically are significant, despite the fact that the paint color in a room might be subtle or even overlooked. Paint is very much like texture in the fact that it can be the finishing touch to make a room perfect, or it can be the final touch that kills a room. If there is only one place in the process that you can splurge and hire a professional, make it be for paint. This might save you a few gray hairs! However, if you are not in a position to hire a professional, that is okay. I have faith in you that you can make a good decision if you take the right steps.

STEP 1

Resist, and resist hard to make any paint selections until all of your other selections in the home are done (flooring, countertops, window treatments, furniture, and the like). You will want to pull inspiration from the finishes and fabrics in a room, so you must have the selections firm.

STEP 2

Remember that paint color is highly subjective, and you are trying to find what color you like best. So take the time to look back at your inspirational images and start to study the various paint colors in the images. Are the walls generally full of color, or are they neutral? Are the trim and ceilings all one color, or are they different colors? Take the time to note what colors work with the trim, versus the built-ins, versus the walls in the inspirational images that just make you feel happy to look at them. Once you have locked onto what it is in these images that takes you to a happy place, do your best to mimic what is happening with the colors in that image. If the images have light walls and dark trim with stained cabinets, or if they have light trim and walls with bold colored cabinets, follow that same pattern with your selections.

STEP 3

Now that you have a plan, it is time to actually make a visit to the paint store. Swatches and fan decks are brilliant, but they are just to be used as a tool in helping you narrow down the types of colors you like. Never, never make a final selection for a color based off of a 1-by-2-inch paint sample! Think about it this way. What if I gave you a 1-by-2-inch picture of someone and asked you to commit to whether or not you could live with them for the next several years based only off that itty-bitty image. Sure, you might be able to determine that they are tall and thin or short and stout, but you would not be able to cypher anything else from that picture—at best, you would be guessing. Paint works the same way. The itty-bitty square of that color will give you a very general idea of what it is, but it will take more investigation to determine if it is the right one for you! So take your plan that you determined in Step 2, visit the paint store, start grabbing swatches of colors that give you the best first impressions, and then move onto Step 4.

STEP 4

Time to narrow down the mountain of swatches you grabbed. Take the swatches you have and start to cut out the individual colors you are really thinking that you like. Now lay out the little cut-out color pieces in the midst of all of either samples, or pictures of all of the selections you have made. For example, for the living room you will want to have a piece of your flooring, images of decorative lighting, swatches of the fabric for things like your window treatments and furnishing, and images or sample chips of the window trim finishes (if they are prefinished). Take all of these samples and lay them out in an area that you can have them and your cut-out paint samples in for a few days. Visit these samples several times during the day to see what colors seem to really be calling your name. You need to have a goal of narrowing it down to three colors for each item needing to be painted (i.e., three for wall, three for trim, three for cabinets, and so forth). When you start to narrow it down, return to the paint store, and order oversized paint samples for these selections (generally, they can be up to 8½ by 11 inches). Getting these oversized paint samples will help you to continue to narrow down before you actually purchase paint.

STEP 5

Samples, samples, samples! Now if providing paint samples was included in the contractor's bid, take the color options you have narrowed it down to, and get the information to the contractor who will be painting your house. Request that they get small pints of paint samples mixed up. If it was not included in their bid, this is a step that you can also easily do yourself. Many paint stores now have inexpensive pints of "paint" that you can purchase for the purpose of testing out colors. Keep in mind that these pints of "paint" are generally not the same makeup as the final paint product you will buy to paint your rooms. They are a cheaper grade of paint, but the color is reliable. Just be sure to not mix the pint of sample paint in with your gallons of final paint that will be used to paint the room.

STEP 6

You or the painters who will be painting your house now need to bust the brushes out and get to work on painting samples. It will be important to not only paint 3-by-3-foot samples on the walls in the specific rooms the colors are possibilities for but also paint on smaller 18-by-18-inch pieces of sheet rock you can carry around with you from room to room.

STEP 7

Now that your samples are complete it is time to study them. The main thing you will be looking for is how does the paint change during the day as the natural light changes? Pay special attention to how it responds to the light in the room during the main times that you will actually be using the room. If you are mainly only home in the evenings, and the paint samples look great all day but start to give off a strange color as the evening approaches, pick another color. It is true that natural light daylight is perfect for getting the real feel of a paint color, but it does you no good to pick it based off of how it looks in natural daylight if you are rarely viewing it in natural daylight. It will be important to take the portable sheet rock samples home and lay your other selection samples (fabric, tile, countertops, and so forth) on the sheet rock and put it under the type of artificial lights you will have in your new home.

STEP 8

After all of that studying, it is time to bite the bullet and pick your colors!

Remember, if you go through all of these steps and you end up not liking a single color you narrowed down to once you have had the chance to study it, do not settle. Just do the steps again, and use the newfound knowledge you have on the colors you do not like. I will be honest—it is hard to get it right the first time, so do not be discouraged to have to re-select. It is worth the hard work now to be happy about the color of room you are in later.

Now you might be thinking, "Thanks for the steps and all, but I am still clueless on what color I like, and just stepping in the paint store makes my heart race with anxiety." Do not fear—I am here to help.

In this case, I would suggest you select neutral paint and stain colors and let your punch of color happen through art and accessories that can easily be swapped out if you get tired of them.

A SIDE NOTE ON PAINT FINISH

Paint generally will come in the following finishes: flat, satin, semi-gloss and glossy. My top choice on paint finish is always flat. If for some reason you are worried about the cleanability of flat paint, then a satin might be a good option. I do not advocate a semi-gloss or glossy paint finish.

A SIDE NOTE ON STAIN COLORS

My best advice is to find a piece of furniture that has the perfect stain color you like and ask the painters to try and make that stain and produce samples for you. Be sure that the painters are producing sample stains for you on the exact type of wood that they will be applied to.

A SIDE NOTE ON HAVING MULTIPLE COLORS

Transitioning from one room to the next with changing paint colors can be tricky. If you do not have the help of a professional, I would make as few color transitions as possible. Bad color changes can disrupt the flow of the house, and it only takes one bad color transition to ruin multiple spaces.